HAMISH MacINNES

HIGHLAND WALKS: FOUR
CAIRNGORMS & ROYAL DEESIDE

'Pleasure is the outcome of exercise'
Motto of Clan MacInnes

D1427791

Hodder & Stoughton
LONDON SYDNEY AUCKLAND TORONTO

Acknowledgments

I should like to thank all the people who helped me with this book and supplied information. For checking it in manuscript I am especially indebted to Libby Whittome, Jim Donaldson, Professor Murdo James MacDonald and his son Alan. My thanks to Graeme Hunter who produced the photographic artwork from my photography and to Alec Spark who drew the maps.

British Library Cataloguing in Publication Data

MacInnes, Hamish
   The roof of Scotland: walks in the
   Cairngorms and Royal Deeside.
   1. Cairngorms (Scotland) –
   Description and travel – Guide-books
   I. Title
   914.12′4   DA880.G7

ISBN 0-340-42384-6

Contents

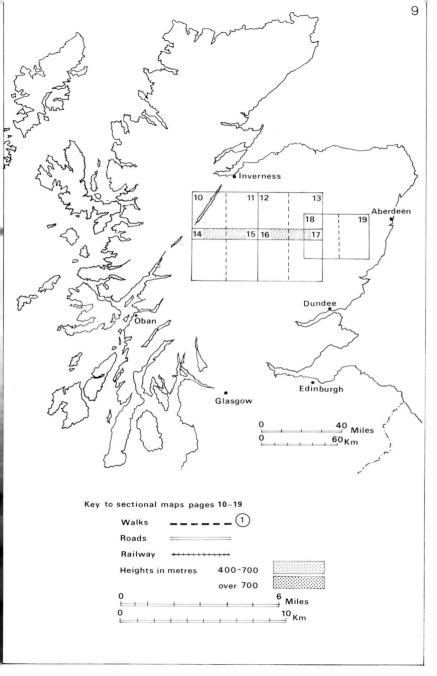

9

Inverness

Aberdeen

| 10 | | 11 | 12 | | 13 | |
| 14 | | 15 | 16 | | 17 | 18 | 19 |

Oban

Dundee

Glasgow

Edinburgh

0   40 Miles

0   60 Km

Key to sectional maps pages 10–19

Walks   ▬ ▬ ▬ ▬ ▬ ①

Roads

Railway   ┼┼┼┼┼┼┼┼┼┼┼┼

Heights in metres   400–700

over 700

0   6 Miles

0   10 Km

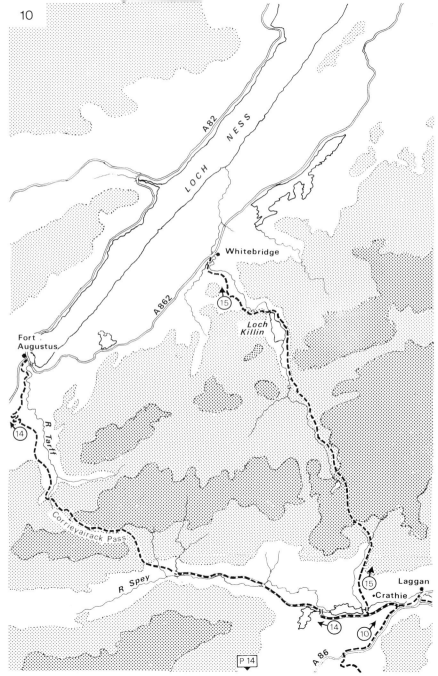

A82

LOCH NESS

A862

Whitebridge

15

Loch
Killin

Fort
Augustus

R Tarff

14

Correyairack Pass

R Spey

15

Laggan

Crathie

14

10

A 86

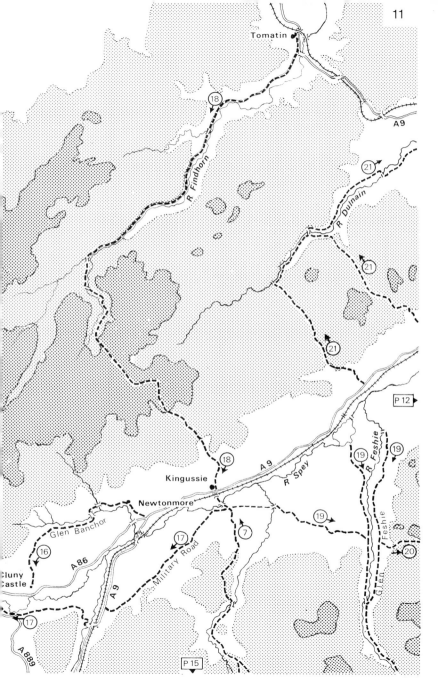

Tomatin

18

A 9

21

R Findhorn

R Dulnain

21

21

P 12

R Feshie

19

19

18

A 9

R Spey

Kingussie

Newtonmore

19

Glen Banchor

17

7

16

A 86

20

Cluny
Castle

A 9

Military Road

Glen Feshie

17

A 889

P 15

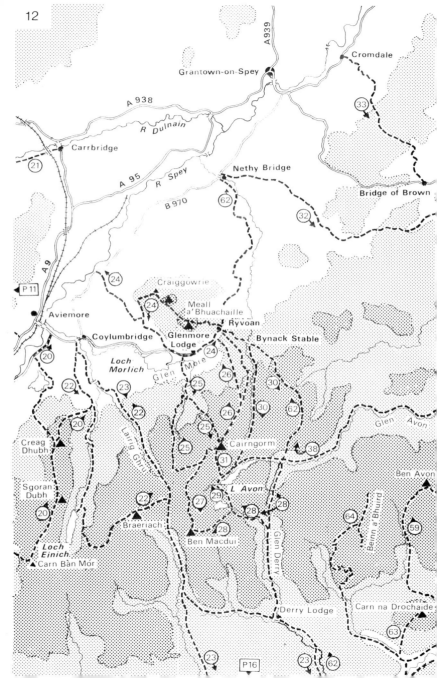

P 11

P16

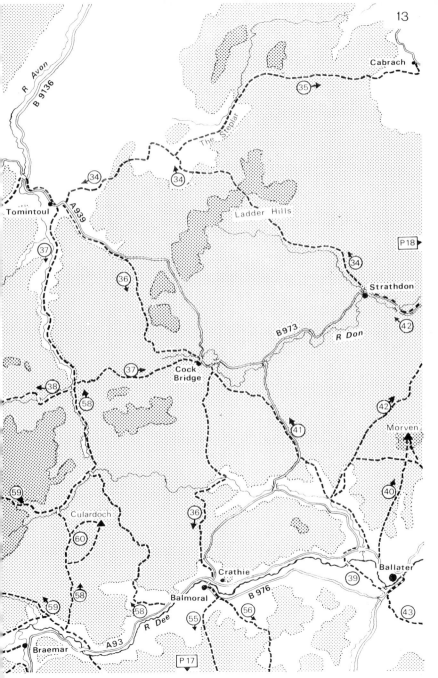

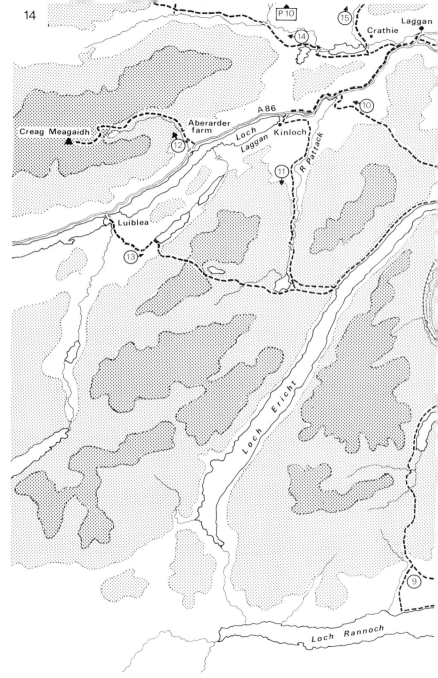

Cluny
Castle
A 86

17

R Spey

A 9

A889

Dalwhinnie

P 11

19

Gaick Lodge

Minigaig Pass

Gaick Path

Dalnaspidal

8

Dalnacardoch

A 9

7

5

Blair Atholl

R Garry

P 16

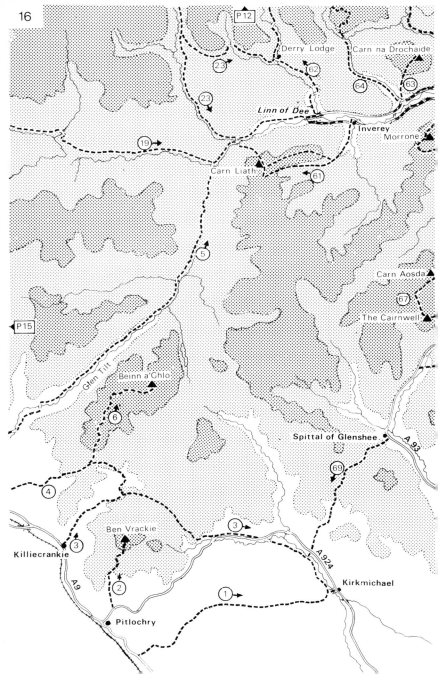

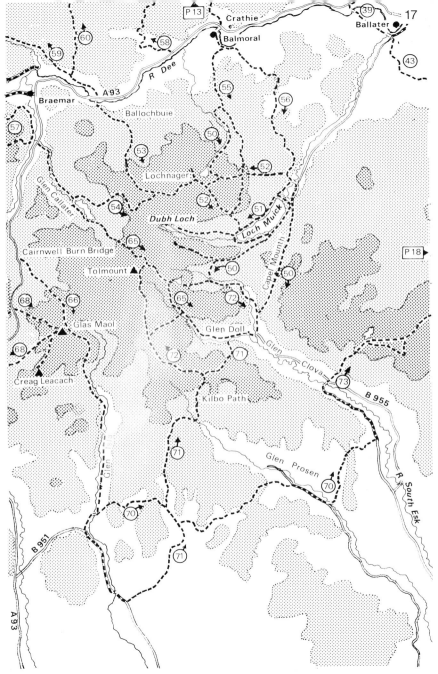

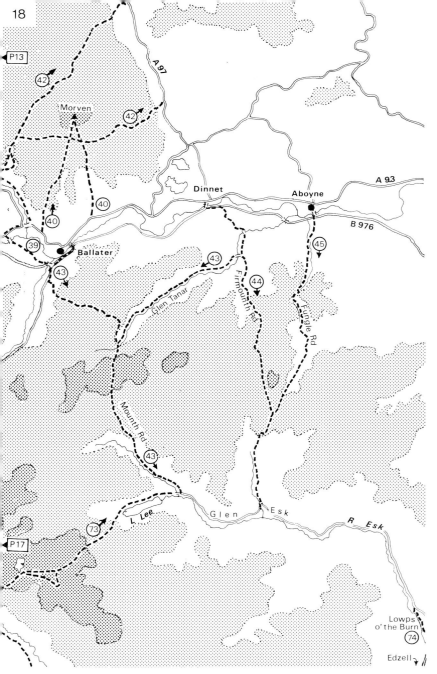

18

P13

42

Morven

42

A 97

Dinnet

Aboyne

A 93

B 976

40

40

39

45

Ballater

43

43

Glen Tanar

43

Firmounth Rd

44

Feungle Rd

Mounth Rd

43

73

L Lee

Glen   Esk

R Esk

P17

Lowps
o' the Burn

74

Edzell

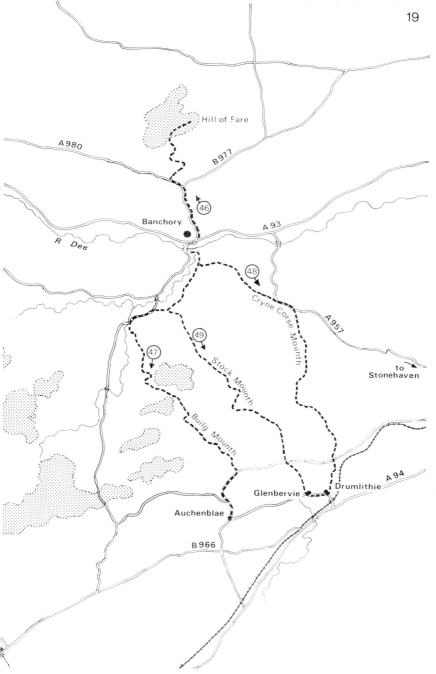

▲ *The Cairngorm ski complex on a typical winter's day.*

Introduction

The Cairngorms represent the highest large plateau area in the British Isles and for several months each winter they are under snow. It is a wonderfully wild country, offering an unrivalled feeling of freedom and space in this now overcrowded world.

Compiling this book I got to know and appreciate these mountains and glens as a walker, rather than as a mountaineer. Here is a region of fine tracks, many originally used by clansmen and drovers; of castles and tales of dispute and strife in harder bygone times. It is an area to savour. It is unique.

Some of the walks described in this book are long and can take you from one side of the range to the other. This means planning in advance how to return to your base, or get to the start. A less athletic but co-operative car-owning friend with time on their hands is a blessing not easily come by; alternatively, you can plan a walk with friends starting at the opposite end and swapping transport temporarily. However, if you are of the true vagabond spirit, not encumbered by vehicles other than those of the public transport variety, your troubles will be minimal, the way long, but the reward just.

Throughout the text I have stressed the danger of going out on to these mountains ill-equipped. Even in summer snow storms can be a hazard and when working on this book in Glen Feshie I was caught in a blizzard with six-foot snow drifts in June. Always take a lightweight anorak and overtrousers with you on the higher walks, plan your route and allow plenty of time.

Naismith's Formula could be a useful starting point for route planning. This states you should allow one hour for every three miles (5km), plus half an hour for each 1000ft (300m) of ascent. This allows time for brief stops for food, but not for sleeping or fishing en route. However, I have purposely omitted estimated times for the various excursions as this book will be used by walkers with a wide variety of ability and times could be misleading. Best to do a couple of the shorter walks first, get yourself fit and see how you shape up for a longer expedition.

A map and compass are essential for all but the simplest hikes and it is equally important to be able to use them correctly. The sketch maps on pages 9–19 are intended only to offer general placing reference and an overall view of the area's potential. Before setting out on any specific walk be sure to equip yourself with the relevant Ordnance Survey maps. The ones recommended to accompany each walk are from the Landranger 1:50 000 series and it is from these that the map references are taken.

The shooting season is from about the beginning of August until the middle of October. If in doubt ask locally. However, the 'closed' season for this book is during snow cover. Don't venture on to the tops if there is snow lying on your planned route.

The area covered by this book is bounded by Pitlochry and Killiecrankie in the south, Tomatin and Grantown-on-Spey in the north, Fort Augustus, Laggan and Dalwhinnie in the west, and Banchory and Auchenblae in the east. Encompassed by these points is the largest group of mountains in the British Isles. Though the Cairngorms is now used as a general term embracing the whole massif, the name properly refers to the dominant hill group which extends from Braemar north to Aviemore and Glen Gairn west to Glen Feshie; 25km south to north and 30km east to west. In fact the true name for this range is Am Monadh Ruadh, the Red Hills. The other great range within the perimeters of this book is the Grampians which extend from Drumochter eastwards to the sea south of Aberdeen. The old name for this group is Am Monadh or, to anglicise the Gaelic, the Mounth. You will find Mounth, meaning hills, cropping up in the name of several of the walks and old roads. Some of these Mounth 'roads' offer outstanding walks, for they are the routes of the clanspeople over and through these mountains. Fir Mounth, Capel Mounth,

Cairn o'Mount, Tolmount – they are names to conjure with and walks which are a must. Throughout the Cairngorms there is a network of good tracks traversing some of the finest scenery in the British Isles. It is a priceless legacy which we have inherited from our forefathers who originally drove their cattle over these remote highways. They are less busy now and it is possible to walk for a couple of days on these tracks without meeting another soul.

I conclude by wishing you as much pleasure as I have had in tramping these hills and glens and visiting the magnificent castles and ancient monuments. This is truly an unspoiled land. Long may it remain so. Scotland's greatest heritage is its wild country, alas a diminishing world asset.

The Pass of Killiecrankie

Where better to start these wanderings on the roof of Scotland than from the Pass of Killiecrankie? The last wolf in Perthshire was killed near here in 1680. Today this narrow defile embraces the A9, the main arterial route to the north about five miles (8km) north of Pitlochry, and is close to the site of a famous Scottish victory in July 1689. James Graham of Claverhouse, 'Bonnie Dundee', led the exiled King James VII's Highlanders and was outnumbered two to one, but defeated the forces of Dutch William III under the command of Major-General Hugh MacKay of Scourie. Two thousand of MacKay's soldiers were killed and five hundred made prisoner.

The battle was not fought in the pass itself, but just to the north. At the council of war before the fight Dundee had been pressed to attack MacKay's force in the confines of the pass, but had declined. It was unfair, he thought, to confront the enemy with such an advantage. However, he paid for this chivalry with his life, falling close to where the main road now runs, mortally wounded through his breastplate. This piece of armour can still be viewed at Blair Castle. As he lay dying by his dun-coloured horse he asked one of his men, "How fares the fight?" On being told, "The day goes well for the King, but I am sorry for your Lordship," Dundee uttered his last words. "It matters less for me, seeing that the day goes well for my master."

The old bridge spanning the River Garry at Killiecrankie was built in 1770 after a ferry disaster in which eighteen people drowned, the ferryman being the only survivor, 'landed' by his wife wielding a boathook. A short distance below the old bridge the river cuts through a cleft and here, close to the Information Centre of the National Trust for Scotland, is the Soldier's Leap. As General MacKay's Williamite army marched through the

◄ *The Pass of Killiecrankie from the north. The site of the battle is beyond the A9 and the vehicle in the middle distance.*

▲ *The Soldier's Leap over the Garry at Killiecrankie.*

pass on that fateful day in 1689 to engage Dundee he left a sentry, one Donald MacBean, a fine swordsman and duellist, to guard the gap. This man was out of sight of the battle, and only aware of his comrades' defeat when he saw a group of clansmen rushing towards him with claymores bared. In a tremendous bound he jumped the seventeen-feet gap above the river and made his escape with news of the defeat.

One mile to the west of the old bridge on the Bonskeid estate, is Coille Bhrochain which means the Wood of Gruel. A plaque on a house gable here commemorates the aftermath of another battle nearly 400 years earlier and records that after the battle of Methven, Robert the Bruce and his hungry and shattered warriors were given a meal of 'brochan' or gruel by the local people.

The Pitlochry/Blair Atholl district is rich in history, and situated on the very edge of gentle country, for north and east the Cairngorms rise steadily to form the highest plateau in the British Isles. There are several worthwhile walks in the Pitlochry area.

Walk 1 Pitlochry to Kirkmichael
OS 52: 960564 to 080601
10 miles (16km)

Go along the Perth road parallel to the A9 for one and three quarter miles and west of Ballyoukan House take the road on the left to the 305m contour where there is a gate. The route continues from here as a wide track. Follow this to crest the shoulder of Faire Mhor where there are a couple of bothies a mile north of Loch Broom. Cut across the rough moors to the east of the buildings to gain Glen Derby. After reaching the Mains of Glenderby it is two and a half miles (4km) to Kirkmichael by the access road.

▼ *The lade and waterwheel of the mill at Pitlochry.*

▲ *The mill workings, Pitlochry.*

Walk 2   Pitlochry to Ben Vrackie
OS 52,43: 944593 to 951633
3 miles (5km) and 2208ft (673m) of ascent

Ben Vrackie, the Speckled Mountain, is Pitlochry's own mountain, the summit of which at 2760ft (841m) commands magnificent views west across the Moor of Rannoch and up Tummel and one feels surrounded by history. A path from Moulin, above the town, climbs some three miles (5km) to Loch a' Choire which nestles just beneath the summit slopes. Another route is from the crest of the Pitlochry/Strathardle road. The three miles from here to the top are pathless. This ascent is approximately 1472ft (448m). A descent route worth recommending is west from the summit to Killiecrankie's wooded depths and the birch trees of Loch Faskally.

Walk 3   Killiecrankie to Kirkmichael
OS 43: 913630 to 081601
16 miles (25km)

Start by the road up the west side of the Allt Girnaig
crossing the fields to Orchilmore, or alternatively from
Aldclune on the road which skirts the site of the Battle
of Killiecrankie. Continue up the glen and take the bridge
over the Girnaig half a mile south of Loinmarstaig. Beyond Loinmarstaig the path turns east to Reinakyllich
after which there is no path, but head east to a point a
mile or so south-east of Shinagag. This is across rough
ground. Continue (hard going) south-east to reach the
Allt na Leacainn Moire and when this stream turns south
through a narrowing on Creag Spardain's east side, ford
it and strike south-east over the crest to drop down to
Glen Brerachan at Dalnavaid (006635), by which time
you will feel you have had a good day. Go east on this
road for two miles (3.2km) and cross the River Ardle to
the Kindrogan road. Following the west side of the river
reach Kirkmichael, passing Dalreoch and Tullochcur-
ran.

Blair Atholl
Blair Atholl owes its historical importance to Blair Castle,
the ancestral home of the Dukes of Atholl. The name
comes from the very old Blar Ath Fhottla meaning Plain
of New Ireland, which goes back to the early Celtic rulers
of Scotland. There have been many additions to the castle
over the centuries, but reputedly the oldest part is the
central tower, Cumming's Tower, which was supposed
to have been constructed by Red Comyn about 1280.

The ancient guest list must read like a Scottish *Who's
Who*. It was here that Viscount Dundee had his council
of war before the Battle of Killiecrankie, and it was in
the church just to the north of Old Blair that he was laid
to final rest after the battle. In 1644 Montrose, that
diligent campaigner, rode up from England with six

followers. At Blair Atholl he found the men of Atholl and Colkitto's Irish ready to set about each other. Montrose called on both forces to join him, which they did, and then marched to victory against the Covenanters at the Battle of Tippermuir. 1653 saw the place stormed by Cromwell's henchmen. In the next century Bonnie Prince Charlie stayed there during the flamboyant early days of the Jacobite Rising of 1745 and saw his first bowling green. After leaving Blair he went a mile or so down the valley to the House of Lude where he appears to have enjoyed himself dancing minuets and Highland reels, requesting one evening 'This is not my ain house'. He visited Blair again the following year and went hunting. The Prince's compass is still at Blair Castle, an instrument which must have been priceless in his later wanderings throughout the Highlands. There is also a set of bagpipes reputedly played by a MacGregor, a piper in the Atholl Brigade during the '45.

Kingsisland is in the Garry about a mile below Blair Castle. According to tradition Robert the Bruce hid on the island after his march down the River Tilt, or possibly a few months earlier after his defeat at Methven. It was here that Bruce's devoted companion, Lord James Douglas, hunted and guddled salmon for the Queen and her ladies.

That trek which the Bruce made from Mar to Blair Atholl provides a fine long walk, taken in reverse. It is sometimes possible to purchase a permit at the estate office, inside the main entrance to Blair Castle, to enable you to drive to Forest Lodge. This cuts down considerably the walking distance to Linn of Dee. It also enables those not so energetic to sample in a more leisurely manner the unique flavour of this Highland glen.

◄ *At Blair Castle is displayed the compass (inset) which Charles Edward Stuart used during the 1745 Rising.*

Walk 4   Blair Atholl to Kirkmichael
OS 43: 879667 to 081601
18 miles (28km)

The route from Blair Atholl to Kirkmichael which joins
up with Walk 3, Killiecrankie to Kirkmichael, offers an
enjoyable day's outing with some fine scenery thrown in.
From Blair Atholl head north (walk or drive) to the Old
Bridge of Tilt and Middlebridge, where there is a signpost
to Strathardle. Continue to the north end of Loch Moraig
where one runs out of public road. A private road continues. Take this to the base of Carn Liath (3197ft/975m)
then south-east to Shinagag where this road ends. Here
the route joins up with Walk 3 from Killiecrankie to
Kirkmichael. A less demanding alternative is to return to
the A9 at Killiecrankie.

Walk 5   Blair Atholl to the Linn of Dee by Glen Tilt
OS 43: 875665 to 062896
27 miles (43km) with 1246ft (380m) of ascent

This old right of way goes up the east bank of the
River Tilt to Fenderbridge. Take to the right at the road
junction on the north side of Fender and beyond, go left
at Kincraigie. This is the end of the public road. Now
cross the hillside and regain the river near Croftmore and
then on to Marble Lodge, an area of fine mixed woodland
scenery, the sort of place where you resolve to return and
linger.

At Marble Lodge you cross the river by the bridge and
follow the west bank of the Tilt.

At the foot of Beinn a' Ghlo, below Forest Lodge on
the north side of the Tilt are the remains of wolf pits. It
is still deer country, however, and patronised by royalty

The old bridge across the River Tilt on the estate road.   ▶

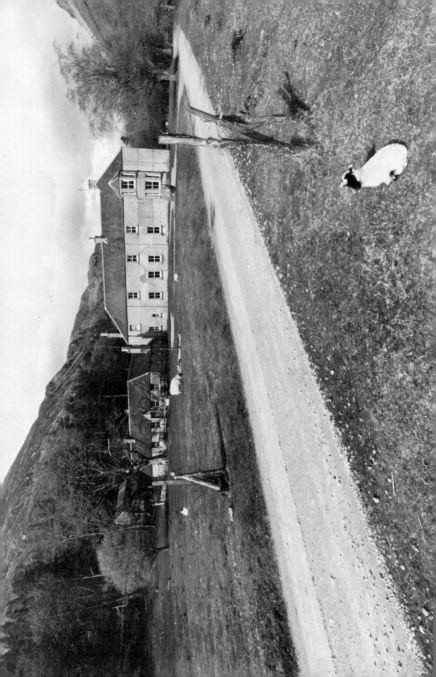

over the centuries. In 1538 James V and Mary of Guise took part in deer drives here, and in 1884 Queen Victoria and the Prince Consort also witnessed a deer drive. While in 1861 they made the long trek that follows from Forest Lodge to Deeside, though probably with ponies.

In 1840 the Duke of Atholl had attempted to close the glen to walkers, but lost this important right of way case. It all started when a Professor J. H. Balfour and a party of botanists returned from an expedition down Glen Tilt and were intercepted by the irate Duke. 'The Ballad of Glen Tilt' commemorates this event:

> . . . The Duke at this put up his birse,
> He vowed in English and in Erse,
> That Saxon fit
> Su'd never get
> Ae single bit
> Throughout his yet,
> Among the Heilan hills, man,
> Balfour he had a mind as weel
> As any Duke could hae, man.
> Quo' he, "There's ne'er a kilted chiel
> Shall drive us back this day, man.
> It's justice and it's public right,
> We'll pass Glen Tilt afore the night,
> For dukes shall we
> Care ae bawbee?
> The road's as free
> To you and me
> As to his Grace himself, man."

The Glen Tilt track was declared a right of way in 1884 by the Court of Session.

The deep trench of the river appears endless after

◀ *Forest Lodge, Glen Tilt.*

▲ *Looking up the Tilt where it passes through a small gorge which was the site of an old bridge.*

Forest Lodge and the terrain becomes starker, but it is not boring, as an urge to see what is beyond lightens your step. The Tilt now squeezes into a rocky gorge and here there is a bridge called Dail an Eas and, a mile and a half beyond, a further bridge close to the junction of the Allt Fheannach which snakes down from Beinn a'Ghlo to the east.

A short way beyond this bridge a Land Rover track goes up left, but the Glen Tilt route carries on by the river to cross the Tarf at Bedford Bridge at the Tarf gorge. Afterwards you ascend steadily up the hillside to the west

The long track up the River Tilt.　　　　　　　　　　　▶

▲ *The Bedford Memorial Bridge across the Tarf Water was erected in 1886 in memory of a young English walker who drowned when attempting to ford the Tarf. The falls above the bridge are worth a visit.*

of the Allt Garbh Buidhe, here running through a rocky cleft, until the slope gives way to a flat open moorland valley. Here there is a feeling of space – this is the real Highlands.

The path now heads towards the remote Loch Tilt, avoiding swampy land, though the loch itself is not visible from this point.

The crest of the pass is reached at 1640ft (502m), and it was here, according to legend, at the watershed of the Tilt and Bynack, that Atholl men are buried. A fight took place when Braemar men attempted to divert the upper Tilt into the Dee, but they were set upon and defeated by Atholl clansmen. Beyond the path dips down to the ruin of Bynack Lodge. Now you must cross the Bynack

Burn which can be dangerous in spate. If it is, stay on the east side of the glen until you reach the footbridge at White Bridge. However, assuming the weather is fair and the level is low, continue across Bynack Burn to the Water of Geldie which you cross by a footbridge to the stable ruins of Ruigh Eallasaid and beyond, the desolate ruins of Ruigh nan Clach. There are superb views on this last section of track on a clear day. From here a rough road leads down Geldie to the White Bridge over the Dee.

On the final stages of this long and satisfying walk, between White Bridge and Linn of Dee are also the ancient ruins of Dubrach. It was a Redcoat outpost after the 1745 Uprising and during this time a sergeant was murdered in the upper reaches of the Allt Cristie. Two men were put on trial five years later at the High Court in Edinburgh for the offence. The court was told by the chief witness for the prosecution that he had been confided in by the ghost of the dead sergeant, who gave him the names of the two accused. When cross-examined by the defence counsel as to what language the ghostly sergeant spoke, the witness responded, "As good Gaelic as myself." The case was laughed out of court.

Peter Grant was the last person to live at Dubrach, and he lived for a long time – for 110 years, dying in 1824. He was the last survivor of the Braemar Jacobites, serving Bonnie Prince Charlie as a soldier. He travelled to Edinburgh in 1822 when he was 108 and was presented by Sir Walter Scott to George IV. The King took him by the hand and stated, "You are my oldest friend." Although Aal Dubrach's immediate retort was "Na, na, yer Majesty, I am yer aaldest enemy," the King granted him a pension of £52 per year and directed that the first payment be made speedily. Braemar Kirk Session made the payments weekly. When Aal Dubrach died his funeral was huge and appropriately the pipers played 'Wha wadna fecht for Charlie'.

Beyond the White Bridge the road sweeps past ruined shielings on green flats, then beneath pines to the gate which marks the start of the public road at the Linn of Dee. A linn, incidentally, is a whirlpool in a deep chasm. From here it is one mile to Inverey and six and a half miles (10.4km) to Braemar.

Walk 6   Blair Atholl to Beinn a' Ghlo
OS 43: 879667 to 970732
9 miles (14km) with 4500ft (1370m) of ascent

Beinn a' Ghlo (3735ft/1129m) is well named the Hill of the Veil or Mist. This is a fine rugged hill, mysterious with its many tops and corries. Some say that there are nineteen corries all told and a gem of information, probably of best use to poachers, is that a rifle fired in any one of them cannot be heard in another.

From Blair Atholl walk or drive up Glen Fender on the road north of Loch Moraig which leads round clockwise into Glen Girnaig. At about 1408ft (429m) you climb quite steeply to the screes of Carn Liath, the Grey Hill (3202ft/975m). (An alternative approach is to take the rough road from Monzie on the north side of the stream to a point three quarters of a mile due west of the summit.) From Carn Liath, the next top to the north-north-east, beyond the col, is a mouthful – Braigh Coire Chruinn-bhalgain, the Upland of the Corrie of Round Little Blisters. One must assume topography rather than chiropody was in the minds of the Gaelic name-givers. Now the route lies east down grassy slopes to the col, Bealach an Fiodha, the Pass of the Timber. From here two streams go their separate ways, one north to Glen Tilt and the other south to Glen Girnaig. The summit of Beinn a' Ghlo which bears the name of Carn nan Gabhar, Hill of the Goats, lies one mile to the north-east.

An alternative route back to Blair Atholl is to descend the north shoulder for one and a half miles, then go west to cross the River Tilt by the footbridge just below where the Allt Fheannach joins it. A word of warning, the Tilt can be dangerous to cross, so use the bridge, and continue down the Glen Tilt track south-west, then south to Blair Atholl.

Walk 7   Blair Atholl to Kingussie by the Minigaig Pass
OS 43, 42, 35: 877665 to 757005
28 miles (44km)

Before General Wade built his road over Drumochter in 1728–9 the Minigaig track over the Mounth to the east was the usual access to the north. This was the only road shown on Green's map of 1689 and Moll's map of 1725, and after Wade's road came into use, the Minigaig was still shown on maps as a 'summer road to Ruthven', i.e. the barracks at Kingussie.

Starting from Blair Atholl follow the east side of the Tilt and cross the Old Bridge to Old Blair. Now follow the Banvie Burn along a rough road and after one and a half miles strike north up the Allt na Moine Baine for three quarters of a mile. Here you cross it and heading north-west go over to Allt ant-Seapail and, still in this same direction, cross to the Allt Sheicheachan which is the termination of the rough road. Still heading north-west follow with care the indistinct path to Glen Bruar, and continue up this glen to Bruar Lodge where the road in from Calvine joins the track (and offers an alternative starting point west of Blair Atholl). Keep to the east side of the Bruar Water for three miles (4.8km) and at the point where the glen branches (819805) go north up the steep face directly ahead, then, slanting slightly right, gain the top of Uchd a' Chlarsair. The path from here to the Glen Tromie road is difficult to follow.

Head in a northerly direction for three miles (4.8km) then at 800887 descend westwards to the Allt Bhran's east bank. (In OS terms you leave the OS 43 to walk a couple of miles across the top right corner of OS 42 before finishing the walk on OS 35.) Follow the rough road down to the junction with the Gaick track (765903), the route from Kingussie to Dalnacardoch.

A mile further north Glen Tromie swings north past Bhran Cottage and just under two miles further on the original route to Kingussie crosses the Tromie by a footbridge short of a wide right-handed bend and climbs northwards across the flank of Sron na Gaoithe to follow the ridge to the west of Tromie for some three miles (4.8km), until you strike the route from Glentromie Lodge running north-west over the shoulder of Beinn Bhuidhe, down into Speyside and the Kingussie road near the Ruthven Barracks.

A popular alternative is to stay on the east bank of the Tromie and continue down the glen as far as the Lodge before crossing the river.

Walk 8   Dalnacardoch to Kingussie by the Gaick Path
OS 42, 35: 723703 to 757005
22 miles (35km) with 576ft (172m) of ascent

This is one of the most interesting of the long-distance routes. The Gaick Forest has an aura of mystery and of danger, too, in winter, being a natural depository for snow blown from the surrounding plateau, which creates an avalanche hazard that has been known to claim both human and animal life.

Begin at the south end of Dalnacardoch, just south-east of the Pass of Drumochter where the A9 has ironed out many of the bends on General Wade's road from Perthshire to Fort Augustus. This part of Wade's original road was completed in 1729 and the celebrations to mark its opening consumed four roast oxen and four kegs of brandy.

General Wade's roads keep getting under our feet in this book. They began as a necessary link between the Hanoverian forts and barracks established to control the

Highlands at Fort Augustus, Bernera in Glen Elg, Ruthven near Kingussie and at Fort William. Only rough drove tracks had existed hitherto, such as the Cateran's Road which ran through the Rothiemurchus Forest and which the Lochaber reivers used on their raids in Banffshire and Moray. So in order to shift the troops needed to keep the Highlanders in their place the General built roads, turning his soldiers to the task of breaching the hill passes of Drumochter and Killiecrankie, building the road from Crieff via the Sma' Glen which encompassed the famous five-arch bridge over the Tay at Aberfeldy, constructing the Corrieyairack, the Slochd and many roads in the west, including the Devil's Staircase in Glencoe, which was completed by General Caulfield. For what Wade began was continued by Clayton, Cope, Caulfield and the famous Thomas Telford. A couple of lines of doggerel sum up his achievements:

If you had seen these roads before they were made
You would lift up your hands and bless General Wade.

This walk begins at Dalnacardoch Lodge. From here take the rough road up Edendon Water to Sronphadruig Lodge. Beyond the glen swings west, but carry straight on northwards on the Gaick path, along the west side of Loch an Duin which lies between the shoulder of An Duin and Craig an Loch's rocky face. Now you can freewheel down past Loch Bhrodainn, along the widening channel of the glen. This loch is named after Brodan, a jet-black hound of Celtic legend who, in the way of such things, came off the worse in a run-in with a demon and pursued a pure white fairy deer into the loch, never to be seen again.

Beyond Loch Bhrodainn cross the footbridge over the Allt Gharbh Ghaig and continue to Gaick Lodge, one of the highest hunting lodges in Britain. Gaick Forest is full of stories, legendary and true. One of the former concerns the famous Witch of Badenoch. A hunter was sheltering from a storm in a lonely bothy with his two dogs when he was disturbed by a scratching at the door. On investigation he discovered a dishevelled cat outside which addressed him in Gaelic as he tried to restrain his hounds from tearing it to bits. This Highland cat confessed that she was a witch who had been ostracised by her professional colleagues for repenting her early misdeeds and had come to the hunter for his sympathy and protection.

The good man (hunters are nearly always good in fairy stories) was an understanding sort of chap and invited her to come in by the fire, but she confessed that she feared his four-legged friends and implored him to tie each of his dogs with a magic hair which she plucked from her head. This he pretended to do, but in fact he just tied them with a slip-knot to a nearby beam.

Thawing out by the fire, the cat gradually grew and took on the form of a woman, and what was more, one the hunter recognised as his respected neighbour, the Good Wife of Laggan. So he was rightly outraged when she revealed her true colours and addressed him, "Hunter of the hills, your hour is come. Long have you been the envy of my sisterhood . . ." After more in this distinctly unneighbourly vein she went for him, but the trusty hounds, not being bound by the magic hairs, leapt to protect their master and in the ensuing fracas tore off one of her breasts. The witch, knowing when to call it a day, transformed herself into a raven and hot-winged it home to Laggan, but not before inflicting fatal injuries on the two dogs who were able to lick the hands of their master before departing to their happy hunting ground.

When the hunter arrived home, a sadder, wiser and dogless man, his wife told him that she had just been at the bedside of the Good Wife of Laggan who had suddenly fallen mortally ill. With purposeful steps the hunter made his way to the Good Wife's house and to the astonishment of the assembled wellwishers, whipped off her bedcovers and revealed for all to see a bleeding breastless crone.

The so-called Good Wife confessed her many misdeeds before she died.

A true, but sombre story of Gaick took place either on Christmas Eve 1799 or in the first week of January 1800, Old Yule according to the early calendar. Five men perished in an avalanche, but at the time it was regarded by many as just retribution for one of them.

Captain John MacPherson of Ballachroan or, as he was known in the Gaelic, Othaichear Dubh (the Black Officer), was a zealous recruiting officer who once even went to the length of arranging a ball to which he invited all the young men of Badenoch, persuading his guests they would cut a much more dashing figure with the ladies wearing King George's uniform. As soon as they put it on they were escorted away and pressed into the army. John MacPherson wasn't the most popular gentleman on Speyside!

On this occasion he and four companions with several powerful dogs set off to the bothy at Gaick to hunt deer. The day after they left a tremendous storm swept the area with heavy snowfall in the mountains. When the hunters didn't return a search party went up to investigate but they could not even locate the bothy on account of the deep drifts. In those days it was beneath a steep slope below Loch an t-Seilich, not at the site of the present lodge.

Next day a larger rescue group went up and found that the bothy had been torn asunder. Large boulders which had formed the walls had been tossed some two hundred yards and the heavy wooden uprights twisted from their positions, "as in breaking a tough stick". From the

The memorial to the avalanche victims, close to the site of the old Gaick Lodge where the Black Officer perished with his fellow hunters. ►

Gaick Lodge from the north, showing the rough road above the shore. ► ►

position of the bodies it appeared that they had been turning in for the night when the avalanche struck. The Black Officer was lying in a prenatal position without his clothes on, still on the remains of the crude bunk; another man was wearing only one sock, as if he had been preparing for bed. The hunters' guns were found in the debris with their barrels twisted by the force of the avalanche. One of the bodies wasn't located until later in the year some distance from the bothy site when the snow melted.

Verses written about this celebrated avalanche offer a warning as applicable today as two centuries ago, for the Cairngorms still claim many victims in winter:

> Awake before your locks are grey,
> Quicken your footsteps on the moor,
> See that your shelter is secure,
> Ere dawneth tomorrow.

In the twentieth century the Gaick area became one of Scotland's first hydro-electric schemes, when water from the Edendon was taken through a tunnel to Loch an Duin and the level of Loch an t-Seilich was raised by a dam built at the north end in 1940. Eleven miles (7km) of tunnel run west beneath the hills to Loch Cuaich and then by an aqueduct to Loch Ericht.

From Gaick Lodge follow the private road along the east side of Loch an t-Seilich to the confluence with the Allt Bhran where the Minigaig Pass track from Blair Atholl joins it from the right. The route now runs down Glen Tromie, a delightful glen, but one which can still live up to its name, Gleann Tromaidh nan Siantan, Glen

The Minigaig path on the left and the Gaick track on the right ▲
from just above their junction in Glen Tilt. Gaick Lodge is beyond the visible road, top right.

The Speyside end of the Gaick walk at Tromie Bridge. ▶

Tromie of the Stormy Blasts. The two alternative approaches to Kingussie are described in Walk 7.

It was at the narrow gorge, Leum na Feinne, or the Fingalians' Leap, that Lord Walter Comyn of Ruthven required the women of Badenoch to work naked in the fields on the day he was due to return from Blair Atholl via the Minigaig Pass. Sadly, the wayward young laird did not live to witness this unusual entertainment, though his mare returned, foaming at the mouth, with one of her master's legs still hanging from a stirrup. A search was instigated for Lord Walter and his remains were found at Leum na Feinne providing a repast for two golden eagles. Until quite recent times there was a curse in Badenoch – *Diol Bhaltair an Gaig ort* (Walter's fate in Gaick on you).

Walk 9   Dalnaspidal to Loch Rannoch
OS 42: 647732 to 617589
12 miles (19km)

Beyond Dalnacardoch the A9 and its companion railway track run over the Pass of Drumochter, at 1508ft (460m) the highest point of the British Rail network. Just south of the pass, at Dalnaspidal, an old drove road runs twelve miles (19km) south-west to Loch Rannoch. Cross the railway at Dalnaspidal Lodge and follow the path over two river bridges and down the west side of Loch Garry to cross the Allt Shallainn. The path leads to a ford, but there is also a footbridge half a mile upstream. After Duinish, continue south to where the way divides, one

General Wade's Stone near the Pass of Drumochter. The ▶
General's men thought this the highest point; in fact the pass is
some miles to the north. The A9 follows long sections of the Old
Military Road.

This is the top of Drumochter Pass, not at General Wade's ▶ ▶
Stone a few miles to the south-east.

Whisky pagodas, the malting houses at Drumochter Distillery. ▶ ▶

route going to Annat, the other to Craiganour Lodge, both on Loch Rannoch. From the north side of Loch Rannoch the B846 joins up with the A9 via Loch Tummel, just south of Killiecrankie.

Dalwhinnie
Dalwhinnie is a whisky village, dominated by its distillery, but it is also conscious now of its tourist potential. The modern visitor certainly fares better than did Queen Victoria and her husband who stayed here, allegedly incognito, in 1861. Their evening repast was described as "supping off two miserable starveling Highland chickens with only tea and without any potatoes and in the morning receiving a visit from Cluny MacPherson". More of the MacPherson clan shortly. Another rather unfortunate visitor to Dalwhinnie was General Johnny Cope, whose army pitched their tents here for one night in 1745. His famous about-turn when confronted by the Jacobites was by the road-end at nearby Dalchully.

Walk 10   Dalwhinnie to Loch Laggan
OS 42, 35: 636862 to 570904
10 miles (16km)

Half a mile north on the Laggan road (A889) a trail runs over to Loch Laggan. You go west on the side of the Allt an t-Sluic for about two miles (3.2km), then north-west up to the pass between Meall nan Eagan and Carn na Ceardaich. Continue north-west into forestry, following the Allt Tarsuinn which you cross, then the River Mashie, to gain the A86 three miles (4.8km) east of Kinloch Laggan.

Cluny MacPherson country
The cliff of Creag Dhubh, the Black Rock, is some three miles (4.8km) south-west of Newtonmore on the Laggan road. It is from this cliff and hill that Clan Chattan took

◄ *Where Water-of-Life is made at Drumochter.*

their war cry, 'Creag Dhubh, Creag Dhubh'. The crest of the clan is the wildcat.

Now Creag Dhubh is best known as a playground for rock gymnasts and wild goats. However, in the past it was famous as the hiding-place of Cluny MacPherson who was a fugitive in the area for nine years after the '45. He was never betrayed by his clansmen, even though there was £1000 on his head and at any one time over one hundred of his men knew where he was holed up, while eighty government soldiers were permanently stationed in the area to harass the clansmen and scour the hills and glens.

Cluny's Cave is high on the right-hand section of the cliff. The small entrance, partly concealed by a triangular rock, can be seen with binoculars from the layby on the A86 close to Lochain Uvie, in which gold coins for the payment of Prince Charlie's forces were said to be hidden after his defeat at Culloden. Two parallel lines of trees cut across the face and the cave is about halfway along the lower edge. Access is up the edge of the forest fence, then over large boulders to gain the margin of the cliff. From here there are old cairns which lead on to the face via a ledge. When the ledge narrows two holes can be seen, which were chimneys for the cave, and just beyond you step down into the rather small boudoir of Cluny, a dwelling of both rising and falling damp. A word of caution, however. The decomposing carcases of sheep at

---

Looking across Lochain Uvie (in which Jacobite treasure is ▶
supposed to be hidden) to Creag Dhubh, a cliff popular with rock climbers. Cluny's Cave is indicated by a circle.

The entrance to Cluny's Cave is at the base of the three trees and ▶ ▶
access is from the top right-hand side of the crag beyond the top left of picture.

A view from the cave looking out to the entrance. Directly above ▶ ▶
is a vent, which acted as a chimney.

▲ *The reconstructed Cluny Castle. The building is not open to the public.*

the bottom of the face on the day I last visited should be a salutary warning to all but the agile.

It is possible that Cluny saw his castle being fired by government troops from his lonely eyrie. For ten years towards the end of the nineteenth century Andrew Carnegie, that Scottish-American tycoon and philanthropist, used to have the shooting tenancy of Cluny Castle which is set back north of the A86 east of Balgowan. He was popular despite his flamboyance, though some of the local worthies didn't appreciate the fact that he flew the Stars and Stripes above the castle.

At the confluence of the Spey and the Truim is the site of the ancient battle of Inverahaven. Here in 1370 the Clan Cameron were to have fought the combined forces of MacPhersons, Davidsons and MacIntoshes. Traditionally the MacPhersons fought on the right wing, but on this occasion they were told that the Davidsons, Clann' ic Dhaidh, were to have that honour. The MacPhersons resorted to industrial inaction instead of arbitration and quit the ranks to partake of a leisurely lunch on a birch knoll. As they ate their oatmeal bannocks they watched the chief of the Davidsons and his seven sons hacked to death. In fact the Davidson clan never recovered from the onslaught and the battle was an overwhelming victory for the Camerons. But there is an interesting sequel. The MacIntosh chief, who had escaped, ordered his bard to compose a satire accusing the MacPhersons of cowardice and then sent him to recite it to the MacPherson chief and say it was a message from Locheil, the Cameron chief. The MacPhersons, incensed at the taunt of cowardice, immediately set off in pursuit of the Camerons.

One of the best preserved Iron Age forts in Scotland is perched on the Black Craig, a wooded rocky outcrop some 600ft high (182m) between the V formed by the junction of the Mashie and Spey (583929). In Gaelic it's

▼ *On the crest of the hill stands what remains of an impressive Iron Age fort, Dun da Lamh, the Fort of the Two Hands. The trees in the foreground were planted to commemorate Cope's Turn on 27th August, 1745, when he decided against meeting Bonnie Prince Charlie's army.*

known as Dun da Lamh, or the Fort of Two Hands, a
name probably implying that one has to climb to get to
it. But it is well worth a visit, and offers a superb view
of the Spey valley. The fortification is irregular in shape.
Part of the wall in the more vulnerable north-west corner
was 25ft thick and estimated to have been 20ft high. The
meticulous dry stone dyking can still be seen in excavated
sections. The remainder of the perimeter is protected by
steep slopes or crags, so easiest access is from the north-
west quarter.

The best way up to the fort is to follow the private road
just south of the bridge across the Spey by the Spey Dam
for half a mile to where a forest road branches right. Go
through a gate and follow the road in a long zigzag to
where it ends at a small clearing south-west of Dun da
Lamh. A path leads above the margin of trees to climb

▼ *The fine stonework of Dun da Lamh.*

▲ *The route up to Dun da Lamh takes the forest road to the left of this notice to a point close to the dun which is at the top of the hill.*

▲ *Dun da Lamh looking west towards the Pass of Corrieyairack.*

▲ *A view down the Spey from Dun da Lamh showing a television relay mast fixed into the old wall of the fort.*

to the saddle, then right through pines to the fort. It is possible to cut out the long zigzag by climbing up the firebreak some 300 yards beyond the forest gate to reach the top end of this road. A further line of approach is up the steep gully on the north side of the saddle, but this is not so convenient. It is amusing to see television relay aerials belonging to residents in the valley within the confines of the ruins.

From Laggan the A86 runs south-west to Loch Laggan. Here a private road on the south side of the loch leads to Ardverikie, a sporting mansion boasting a great deer forest. Queen Victoria stayed at Ardverikie on her first visit to the Highlands and Prince Albert stalked the Ben Alder corries. Upon being introduced to the Queen, the

Looking down on the Spey Dam from Dun da Lamh. ▲

The fairytale architecture of Ardverikie across Loch Laggan. The ▶
site has roots deep in Scottish history.

young son of her host, the Marquis of Abercorn, persisted in standing on his head. As he was wearing the kilt, he did not endear himself to that formidable lady.

The name Ardverikie is a corruption of Ard Fergus and indeed there is a mound in the garden reputed to be the grave of King Fergus of Dalriada who died in AD 501, long before Kenneth MacAlpine united the Picts and the Scots. Two islets in the loch nearby are said to have been the sites of Fergus's hunting-seat and his kennels.

Walk 11   Kinloch to Dalwhinnie by the Pattack valley
OS 42: 538897 to 635850
16 miles (25km) with 350ft (106m) of ascent

From just west of Kinloch in the Ardverikie estate a route goes up and over to the Pattack valley, continues past Loch Pattack, and sweeps round through the Ben Alder Forest to Ben Alder Lodge on Loch Ericht. The road then follows the north-west shore of Loch Ericht to Dalwhinnie.

An alternative start to this walk is to go east from Kinloch for two miles (3.2km) and branch right to Gallovie (552891). Follow the forest road to Linn of Pattack and the River Pattack to where the path comes over from Kinloch.

Further west along the A86 is Aberarder Farm, now a nature reserve. This is the start of the access route into Creag Meagaidh, one of Scotland's great winter climbing corries. Late spring is the best time to view the imposing cliffs, whilst they are still shrouded in the winter snows.

◀ *From the bridge at Lochan na h-Earba with the crags of Binnein Shuas behind. This is a popular playground for rock climbers with probably the best known climb, Ardverikie Wall, going up the whitish line just right of centre on the face.*

Walk 12   Aberarder Farm to Creag Meagaidh

OS 42 or 34: 479876 to 418876
4 miles (6km) with 1100ft (335m) of ascent

The path starts from the farm buildings (479876) and
follows the stream for four miles (6.4km) into the corrie.
From Lochan a' Choire, the loch at the foot of the cliffs,
it is possible to skirt right to gain the Window (426886),
a pass to the north of Creag Meagaidh. Through here in
August 1746 Prince Charles Edward Stuart made his way
after his flight from the Isle of Skye, and at Aberarder
received the 'short brown coat' he so badly needed.
Afterwards he hid in Cluny's Cage on nearby Ben Alder,
where he received the news that a French vessel had
arrived at Loch na Uamh on the western seaboard to take
him back to France. It is best to return to Aberarder from
the Window by the same route but, if conditions are
suitable, you can make the ascent of Creag Meagaidh
(3706ft/1130m). The ascent is easy and the summit is one
mile from the edge of the corrie. Descent can be back to
the Window or to the east down the ridge to the farm. It
should be noted that many climbers go astray on this
mountain in bad visibility and often end up in Glen Roy.
As with other hill walks in these mountains, a map and
compass are essential and it's equally essential to be
competent in their use.

Loch Laggan and Loch Moy are connected by a short
channel over which a Forestry Commission bridge allows

Aberarder, the start of a fine walk into Creag Meagaidh, a route ▶
which Charles Edward Stuart took in August 1745.

Coire Ardair of Creag Meagaidh, with the 'posts', the steep snow ▶ ▶
gullies in the centre of the face. The Window is the pass on the
right, over which Charles Edward Stuart travelled.

Loch Laggan from close to Kinloch Laggan. The track in the ▶ ▶
foreground goes over the hill to near Garvamore.

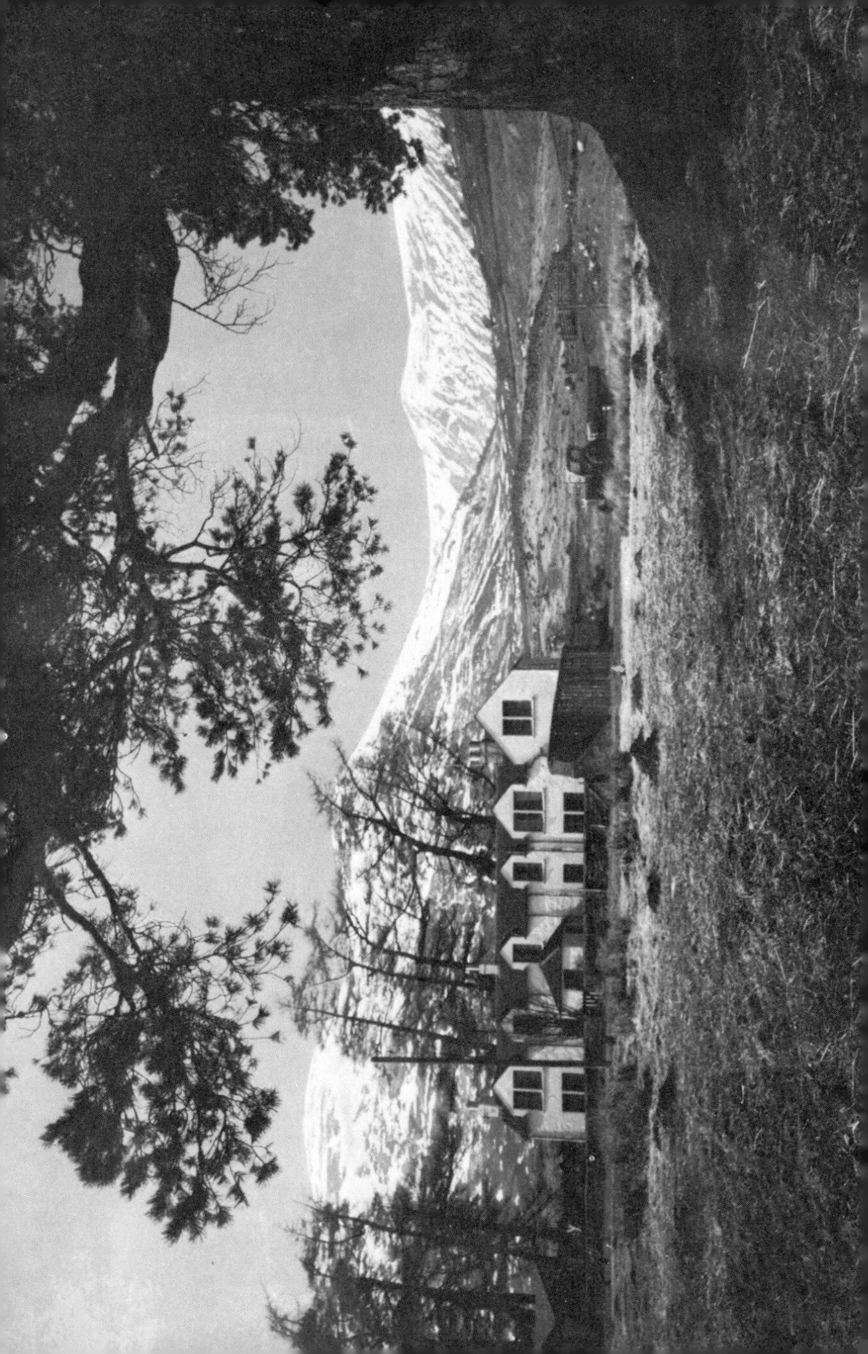

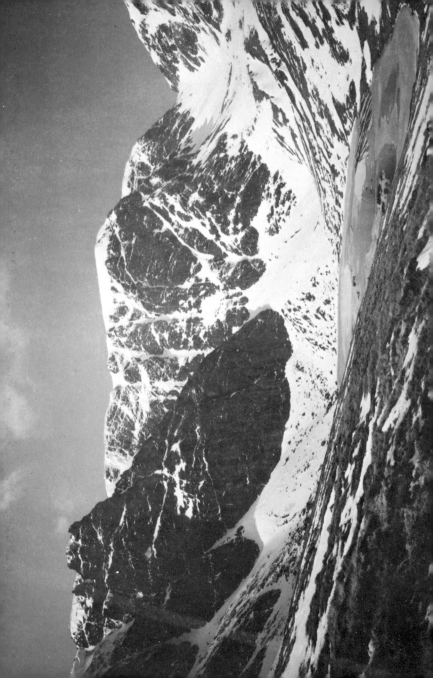

access to the wild area of Ben Alder Forest. From here a walk of some nineteen miles (30.4km) takes one to Dalwhinnie, joining the track from Kinloch en route. So it is also possible to make a round trip, reversing Walk 11 from Loch Pattack, and exit at Kinloch Laggan.

Walk 13   Luiblea to Dalwhinnie
OS 42: 433830 to 635850
19 miles (30km)

From the bridge at Luiblea a Land Rover track goes to the south-west end of Lochan na h-Earba, from where you follow the Allt Coire Pitridh to the south side of Loch a' Bhealaich Leamhain. Descend to the Allt Cam and Loch Pattack, skirting the southerly shore of the latter to join up with the Ardverikie track. Continue, as for Walk 11, on to Ben Alder Lodge and Dalwhinnie. Alternatively, turn northwards at Loch Pattack for Kinloch Laggan.

Corrieyairack
One of the most famous of all Highland walks is the Corrieyairack. This is a General Wade road of some twenty-five miles (40km) from Laggan to Fort Augustus. The road was constructed in 1731 and is a continuation of his military road from Crieff to Dalwhinnie via Dalna-cardoch and the Drumochter Pass. At Dalwhinnie it branches, one road going to Inverness via Aviemore and the other by Laggan across the Corrieyairack to Fort Augustus. There was a road of sorts over the Corrieyairack before the pick-and-shovel General came on the Highland scene. One was shown on a map of 1725, but it was probably no more than a track.

It took 500 soldiers to build the Corrieyairack road and at an altitude of 2507ft (764m) the pass seems to collect bad weather, especially in the winter months. There is record of a mother who perished here while her baby survived. It was found covered by snow and nursed back to health by the Governor's wife at Fort Augustus. There are tales too of soldiers dying on the pass: "They over-refreshed themselves with whisky before the climb."

Prince Charles Edward Stuart and his Highlanders marched from Fort Augustus to the pass at the end of August 1745. He had received word that General Cope was encamped at Garvamore on the Speyside side of the pass and that morning, when he put on a new pair of brogues, he stated: "Before I throw these off I shall meet with Mr Cope."

The Prince dispatched a reconnaissance party to the summit of the pass but they reported back that not a creature was to be seen. Later in the day forty deserters from Cope's forces were spotted ascending the zigzags to join the Jacobite cause. Cope meantime had thought it wiser to opt out and had headed post haste for Ruthven and Inverness. A clump of trees close to Dalchully commemorates 'Cope's Turn'.

Walk 14   Laggan to Fort Augustus by the Corrieyairack Pass
OS 35, 34: 615944 to 375084
25 miles (40km) with 1404ft (427m) of ascent

From the A86 at Laggan it is possible to drive the first few miles along General Wade's road, past Dalchully House and the Spey Dam.

Now a tarred road goes beyond the old barracks and inn at Garvamore, over the elegant Garva Bridge to near Melgarve. This is as far as one can drive. From here the

Garvamore Barracks, used by the troops building the road in 1732, and later as a drovers' inn. It was also frequented by the King's troops crossing the Corrieyairack Pass who "often perished there by imprudently drinking quantities of spirits at the inn on the moor, thinking thereby to keep out the cold; but, alas it was sure way to destruction."

Garva Bridge on Wade's road en route to the Pass of Corrieyairack.

track (it was 14–15ft wide when General Wade made it) climbs by the Allt Yairack, snaking up the twelve zigzags in 500ft (152m) to the summit at 2507ft (764m). It dips steeply down the Fort Augustus side to Lagan a' Bhainne Bridge, then Glen Tarff to Culachy. When you gain the public road go right then first left to Fort Augustus.

This is a superb walk with fine views. There is a steep descent on the wide side to Lagan a' Bhainne Bridge and Glen Tarff. The summit of the Corrieyairack Pass is exposed and, like the other passes in the region, subject to snowstorms in spring, autumn and winter.

An alternative start to this walk is from close to the filling station just west of Kinloch Laggan. Follow the rough track over the hill into Glen Shirra to join Wade's road at the canal bridge east of Glenshero Lodge (553933).

Walk 15 Crathie to Whitebridge
OS 35, 34: 583935 to 485152
22 miles (35km)

Start from Crathie by the Spey Dam just west of Laggan to follow this route over to Whitebridge on another stretch of General Wade road, now the A862. Go north up Glen Markie to just beyond Piper's Burn which joins the true right of the Markie Burn, then ascend to the north-west to the east end of Lochan a' Choire. There is no path for this section. After cresting the ridge, head for the north end of Loch na Lairige to take the east bank of the Crom Allt and a path which runs down to Sronlairig Lodge. Follow the rough road down the River Killin, past Loch Killin and on to Whitebridge.

Newtonmore

Newtonmore is a popular all-year-round holiday village. Since it was bypassed by the new A9 highway, its richly deserved air of tranquillity is only broken during the

Looking back down the track of the Corrieyairack to Melgarve ▶
at the end of the public road.

shinty season while the local team preserves the best championship record in Scotland. The game, not unlike Irish hurling, is played with sticks called camans on a pitch up to twice the area of a football field, and its ancient roots are reputed to be in the battle training for Celtic warriors.

Newtonmore is situated on the doorstep of the Monadh Liath Mountains, where the Truim and Calder join forces with the Spey. Glen Banchor, down which the Calder flows, strikes north then west from the village, while Glen Truim runs south accompanied by both the railway and the A9 to breach the Pass of Drumochter.

The Clan MacPherson has its clan museum at Newtonmore and this is well worth a visit on a day not suitable for hills and glens; indeed it is a worthwhile visit any day. Here you can see the famous fiddle of James MacPherson who was hanged for cattle reiving in Banff on 16th November, 1700. It is reported that the town council put the clock forward to forestall an expected reprieve. On the gallows MacPherson offered his fiddle to any onlooker who would take it, but as there were no takers he broke it in pieces, after playing the famous tune now known as 'MacPherson's Rant'. The following verses commemorate the occasion:

> There's some cam' here to see me hanged
> And some to buy my fiddle,
> But before that I do part wi' her
> I'll brak' it through the middle.
>
> He took the fiddle into baith of his hands,
> And he broke it ower a stane.
> 'There's nae ither hand shall play on thee
> When I am dead and gone.'
>
> O little did my mither think
> When first she cradled me
> That I would turn a rovin' boy
> And die on the gallows tree.

The reprieve was coming ower the brig o' Banff
To let MacPherson free.
But they pit the clock at a quarter afore
And hanged him to the tree.

Unlike MacPherson, the fiddle could be salvaged and the pieces were stuck together again and find their place in the museum along with Prince Charlie's blanket and the famous Black Chanter, the Feadan Dubh of the MacPherson clan, dropped, by all accounts, from heaven at the battle of North Inch of Perth in 1396.

Walk 16   Newtonmore to Cluny Castle by Glen Banchor
OS 35: 712992 to 645944
10 miles (16km)

Here is a relatively easy walk from Newtonmore. Go up the north side of the River Calder to Glenballoch and cross the river at Keppel Bridge (678988), one mile further on. Now follow the south side of the river for about one and a half miles to gain Strath an Eilich and take this in a southerly direction to Cluny Castle. From here it is a mile and a half to Laggan along the A86.

Kingussie
Close to the A9, Kingussie is a popular all the year round centre for winter sports and fishing, or for the network of walks fanning out from the valley of the Spey. Nearby, across the river, is Ruthven Barracks. In the sixteenth century this was the site of a Gordon castle, and before that it was one of the fortresses of a son of Robert II, Alexander Stewart, the infamous Wolf of Badenoch, who burned Elgin Cathedral. Ruthven Castle itself was burned in 1689 by Bonnie Dundee before being rebuilt as a barracks for government troops in the anti-Jacobite campaign. The remnants of the Young Pretender's forces reassembled at Ruthven after their disastrous defeat at Culloden. When they left they also burned it.

At the north end of the town is the Am Fasgadh Folk

Museum, a place well worth visiting, not just on a wet afternoon. While the old graveyard at Mill Road boasts an unusual Celtic recess in the north walling where a notice states: "Here is the hallowed site of the old church of Kingussie, dedicated to St Columba and, according to tradition, planted by himself." Then in Gaelic is added, "My Druid is Christ the Son of God." A clear case of the Celtic missionaries making a pitch for the incumbent religion.

Walk 17   Kingussie to Laggan by a military road
OS 35: 756004 to 615944
15 miles (24km)

Cross the Spey from Kingussie by the B970 to Ruthven Barracks, then go in a south-westerly direction along General Wade's road to Milehouse of Nuide, Lochan Odhar and Phones. (Here it is possible to cut the walk short by heading north-west to gain the A9.) Continue until you come to Etteridge which is the key to crossing the A9 and the railway line and then the River Truim to reach Crubenbeg. Now take a track north then west which skirts the hillside above the Spey to arrive at Catlodge on the A889. Laggan is two miles along the A889.

Walk 18   Kingussie to Tomatin by the River Findhorn
OS 35: 755015 to 803289
27 miles (43km)

Start up the road by the golf course and follow the Allt Mor to the low part of the ridge between Carn an Fhreiceadain and Carn a' Bhothain Mholaich. Don't follow the stream on the other side of the ridge, but head north-west to the next stream, the Allt Ghlas a' Charbaid. There is no path here, so take care in mist. Follow this

◄ *Ruthven Barracks, Kingussie.*

A black house at the Highland Folk Museum, Kingussie.   ►

stream down to the north to reach the Elrick Burn, then Coignafearn Lodge. From here take the minor road that runs all the way along the Findhorn to reach Tomatin. The Findhorn is one of Scotland's most spectacular rivers and the final leg to Tomatin quiet and scenic. If tarmacadam, even at its least objectionable, is unacceptable, exercise your logistical ingenuity in organising someone to pick you up with a car at Coignafearn Lodge.

◄ *The approach to the Pictish weem, the Cave of Riatts, across the A9 (left) from Lynchat. The cave is located near the centre of the photograph.*

▼ *The Cave of Riatts, looking back down to where the previous photograph was taken at the corner of the field.*

▲ *Inside the Cave of Riatts.*

Some two miles (3.2km) east of Kingussie is the Cave of Riatts, or MacNiven's Cave. At one time the local MacNivens fell out with the Clunys (Clan Chattan) over maltreatment of a Cluny daughter whose petticoats were cut off with a dirk and, to add insult to injury, so was the tongue of Cluny MacPherson's cherished bull. So the MacPhersons (Cluny) descended on the MacNiven homestead one night and murdered everyone they could lay their hands or claymores upon. However, eighteen survived by hiding in a secret cave beneath the floor. This man-made cave (a Pictish weem 40ft by 8ft and 6ft high) can still be seen in a field close by the A9 to the west of the hamlet of Lynchat and is labelled 'Souterrain' on the OS 35, at 777019. It can be awkward to find, but well worth a visit. A small road runs north from the east side of Lynchat. Take this for a short way and go under the A9 via a large culvert. On the other side of this follow the Land Rover track parallel to the main road to a field gate. Look for the weem on rising ground where some humps are visible near the middle of the field.

The B970 is a road which seems to have plenty of time. It takes a leisurely route on the south side of the Spey offering an abundance of scenery; trees, river and moun-

SACRED
TO THE MEMORY OF
MY ADORED HUSBAND
HENRY EDWARD
BREWSTER MACPHERSON
OF BALAVIL
ENTERED INTO HIS REST
ON 24TH NOVEMBER, 1946

"HIS LOVE TO ME
WAS WONDERFUL"

tain. Loch Insh, with its birch-lined banks, is one of the finest lochs in the area, even if it is only a natural widening of the river, famous for its fishing and, nowadays, as a centre of wind surfing and canoeing. The name is derived from the Gaelic *innes*, referring to the high pine-crowned mound of land at the north end, Tom Eonain, which was once an island. Here, on a Celtic site dating from the sixth century, the ancient parish church is well worth inspection. The mound is called after Adamnan, the biographer of Columba. His handbell is still here and is reputed to possess a supernatural self-recovery system, for when it was stolen, it allegedly flew back to Tom Eonain from the Pass of Drumochter intoning, "Tom Eonain, Tom Eonain" the while. The church and its surrounding graveyard, like so many in Scotland, is on a site conducive to worship and contemplation.

Walk 19   Glen Feshie to the Linn of Dee
OS 35, 43: 790995 or 836038 or 854044 to 062896
32 miles (51km)

This is one of the most picturesque long walks in the Cairngorms. The crowded lower forestry planting leads beyond to the splendour of isolated Caledonian pines which to me is Highland landscape at its best.

There is a choice of three starting points for this walk down Glen Feshie and the combination also offers an agreeable shorter circuit walk for those based on Speyside with more modest walking ambitions. First, from Tromie Bridge (790995), and Drumguish, the path goes up over Forestry Commission land to the bridge over the Allt Chromhraig, then on east across open moorland via

◄ *The MacPherson family obelisk (behind) depicting James 'Ossian' MacPherson is across the A9 from his home at Balavil. In one of the greatest literary con tricks MacPherson 'translated' the Gaelic verse of Ossian, and inspired thereby such men as Goethe and Napoleon. MacPherson died in 1796 and was buried in Westminster Abbey.*

Corarnstilmore and through more forestry to reach Glen Feshie. Here the route meets up with variant two, the road south from Insh House (836038). There is vehicular access for three miles along this road as far as Tolvah. Our third starting point is from Feshie Bridge (854044) and up the east side of the Feshie via Lagganlia, turning right alongside the landing strip, then following close to the river as far as Achlean where the road ends. (There is a nature trail here in the old Caledonian wood of Badan Mosach.) Our route continues, however, close to the river, and all three routes unite at the bridge at Carna-chuin. This is the point for those who do not wish to continue east to Braemar to pick one of the alternative ways back to Speyside.

The more determined should now cross to the east bank of the river. Here an estate road runs temptingly up eastwards, following the Allt Coire Chaoil and giving access to the peaks and plateau above. But our Glen Feshie to Braemar route still follows the river through magnificent Caledonian pines. It passes close to the bothy of Ruigh-aiteachain. In another now ruined bothy nearby Landseer, a frequent visitor to Glenfeshie Lodge, painted a fresco which was still discernible above the fireplace until 1930. The path beyond the bothy has been damaged in places by landslides. Some seven miles (11km) from the Carnachuin bridge there is a fork in the path at a bothy. Go left to a bridge half a mile up the River Eidart at 914887. After the bridge, where the glen swings round, our track goes uphill and to the east to cross the divide to gain the north bank of the Geldie Burn. In three miles (4.8km) the ruin of Geldie Lodge is reached and a further three miles on the Glen Tilt to Linn of Dee route described in Walk 5. From the Linn of Dee a minor road runs seven miles (11km) on to Braemar.

▲ *A division of the ways in Glen Feshie.*

◀ *Feshie Bridge.*

▲ The bridge across the Feshie close to Feshie Lodge. On the other side the path continues upstream, passing the mountain bothy in which Landseer used to paint.

▲ *The junction of the ways: Glen Feshie, Glen Tilt and the way to Braemar.*

▲ *The wonderful Caledonian pines of Glen Feshie.*

▲ *The bothy of Ruigh-aiteachain, Glen Feshie.*

▲ *Here Glen Feshie swings round to the east; one of the finest of Cairngorm glens.*

Walk 20　Glen Feshie to Carn Ban Mor and Creag Dhubh
OS 36: 852976 to 915108 or 890098
4 miles (12km) with 2200ft (670m) of ascent

This fine walk north along the tops begins by going south up Glen Feshie along the route of Walk 19 as far as the road-end at Achlean. Here follow a rough road uphill, which brings you on to the Foxhunters' Path up the north side of the Allt Fhearnagan, the Burn of the Little Alder Place. Follow up Coire Fhearnagan to 3378ft (1029m) to gain the plateau to the south of the summit, the source of the Allt Fhearnagan, which is a little depression that retains snow until late in the year. It is called Ciste Mearaid, Margaret's Coffin or Chest. The Margaret in question is English Queen Margaret who married Malcolm Canmore in the eleventh century.

From the summit of Carn Ban Mor (3450ft/1052m), the Big Fair Hill, it is possible to traverse the peaks to the north. First comes Sgor Gaoith (3667ft/1118m), the Peak of Wind, then Sgoran Dubh Mor (3648ft/1111m). Beyond this peak you pass Sgoran Dubh Beag at the cliff edge. Continue northwards and shortly a path can be followed which takes you to a col at 2497ft (761m) just to the west of Coire Cregach nam Bo and Lochan Beanaidh. Continue on to the flat top of Creag Dhubh. Here there are two tors. The first is Coutts Stone, Clach Choutsaich, and the next the Argyll Stone, Clach Mhic Cailein. Follow on over Cadha Mor, then north-east to join the Gleann Einich track in to Coylumbridge via Whitewell. An alternative for this final descent from Creag Dhubh is to branch north-west towards Creag Fhaiclach to join a path at 900046. Follow the Allt Coire Follais and then on down to the Land Rover track to the south of Loch an Eilean, and so round the loch to the B970 at Doune.

▼ *The twisted branch of a Caledonian pine, Glen Feshie.*

Loch an Eilean Castle, built by the Wolf of Badenoch. The loch was dammed over 200 years ago and the water used for floating timber to the Spey. Nearby was a boring mill, where logs were bored for use as water pipes.

Loch an Eilean, Loch of the Island, is one of the jewels of Rothiemurchus, set amidst Caledonian pines with the backdrop of the Cairngorms beyond. It is difficult to imagine how such a setting could be improved upon. The island which gave the loch its name is the site of a ruined castle, possibly dating from the fourteenth century, as it is reputed to have been built by the Wolf of Badenoch, Alexander Stewart, Earl of Buchan. But it was most likely a Comyn stronghold before then. It was built round a courtyard with a square keep, high curtain walls and lesser flanking towers. According to tradition, a secret zigzag underwater causeway linked it to shore. The three murderers of the head of Clan MacIntosh were imprisoned here for seven years in the sixteenth century before being brought to trial and found guilty. The leader was be-headed and quartered. The other two were tortured, then hanged, and their heads were cut off and set upon spikes at the scene of the crime.

On a gentler note, the island was once a favourite nesting place for the osprey. Today Loch an Eilean boasts a Tourist Information Centre and an old limekiln near the car park, and there is a fine nature trail round the loch. From the western shore you can hear a triple echo and obtain a splendid view from Ord Ban, the Fair Round Hill.

Between Loch an Eilean and its smaller neighbour, Loch Gamhna, is the old Thieves' Road, the Rathad nam Meirleach, used by clansmen reiving cattle in the fertile lands of Moray. It started from Lochaber in the west and eventually wound its way through Rothiemurchus, along the south side of Loch Morlich and on to An Lochan Uaine, the Green Loch, and Ryvoan. But it can now only be traced on the shore of Loch Gamhna, the south sides of Loch an Eilean and Loch Morlich.

Inverdruie, close to one of the northern turnoffs for Loch an Eilean was at one time the centre of a large timber operation where logs were assembled for rafting down the Spey. Today there is a Visitors' Centre here offering guided tours around the Rothiemurchus estate. The name Rothiemurchus means the Great Plain of the Firs. Between Inverdruie and Loch an Eilean is the house of Tullochgrue where Lord 'Lewie' Gordon, one of the last of the 1745 fugitives, was sheltered by the laird's wife. Rothiemurchus has been in the possession of the Grants of Rothiemurchus for 400 years. A daughter of the house was Elizabeth Grant, author of *Memoirs of a Highland Lady*, a graphic account of life in the late eighteenth century. In her writings she mentions a Grant called Black Sandy, who cut off the ear of a maiden for reasons into which we shall not delve. To avoid punishment he hot-footed it to North America and his son, Ulysses Grant, was commander of the successful Union forces during the American Civil War, and later President of the United States.

◄ *An old lime kiln, Loch an Eilean.*

Aviemore

Aviemore, or Agaidh Mhor, which is Gaelic for Big Face, used to be no more than a stagecoach inn. Later it seemed to crowd round the railway station, for many years the focal point of the village. Aviemore clung on to its village status until the 1960s when the economic value of lots of snow was realised. Before then the vast acres of woodland in the Rothiemurchus and Glenmore forests, and on Deeside, were a source of employment and of revenue for generations. Thomas Pennant, writing in 1771, recorded trees "from 80 to 90 feet high, without a lateral branch and 4½ feet in diameter at the lower end". Even in 1834 the annual timber revenue from the Rothiemurchus estate was in the region of £20,000. The logs used to be floated down to the Moray Firth by a combination of dams and sluices in the side valleys, then rafted down to the mouth of the Spey, guided by men in curraghs and control ropes to the banks. Elizabeth Grant of Rothiemurchus records one particular hazard near Ardnilly in lower Strathspey in her *Memoirs of a Highland Lady*.

> Near Ardnilly there was a sunken rock difficult sometimes to pass; this furnished a means of livelihood to several families living on the spot. It was their privilege to provide ropes, and arms to pull the ropes, and so to help the floats through a rapid current running at high floods between this sunken rock and the shore. The dole they got was small, yet there was hardly more outcry raised in Sutherland when the Duke wanted his starving cottars to leave their turf huts on the moors and live in comfortable stone houses by the sea, than my father met when some years later he got leave to remove this obstacle by blasting.

This timber work was seasonal. Where Aviemore station now stands there used to be a bothy for the 'floaters' as they were called.

Now winter skiers and summer tourists arrive all the year round by train from the south to find themselves in a village turned tourist complex with the vast backcloth

▲ *Aviemore with the Cairngorms beyond.*

of the Cairngorms to the south-east. Aviemore has become an all-the-year-round centre with a great wealth of activities to offer, both indoors and out, and on the doorstep is an enormous range of mountains.

From just behind the Aviemore Centre there is a gentle hill walk to the top of Craigellachie, Rock of the Stony Place, one of the best viewpoints over the Spey valley and the Cairngorms. The name is incorporated in the war cry of Clan Grant, "Stad, Creag Eileachaidh!" (Stand fast, Craigellachie). Go via the peaceful Loch Pulladdern and on into the Craigellachie birch wood, a national nature reserve with a nature trail which offers a forty-minute walk. A couple of miles down the Kingussie road from Aviemore is Loch Alvie where at the nearby little white Kirk of Alvie (864094) 150 uncoffined skeletons were discovered under the floor when the building was restored in the 1880s. They were reinterred in the kirkyard with the following stone inscription:

BURIED HERE
ARE
REMAINS OF 150 HUMAN BODIES
FOUND OCTOBER 1880
BENEATH THE FLOOR OF THIS
CHURCH.
WHO THEY WERE
WHEN THEY LIVED
HOW THEY DIED
TRADITION NOTES NOT

Their bones are dust, their good swords rust,
Their souls are with the saints, we trust.

The church was again renovated in 1952 by Sir Basil Spence, architect of the new Coventry Cathedral.

Walk 21   Aviemore to Carrbridge by the River Dulnain

OS 35, 36: 882108 or 844073 to 906230
17 miles (27km)

Just before Loch Alvie, the turning at Easter Lynwilg is the starting point for this walk. Follow the track north-west by the north bank of the Allt Dubh. Then cross the ridge to the north of Geal-charn Mor. Disregard rough road turnings to the left and follow a route to the north-west down to the bridge over the River Dulnain. Now continue north-east down the west side of the river for four miles (6.4km) to the bridge (not shown on OS 35) at Dalnahaitnach and then take the opposite bank on to Carrbridge.

Alvie Lodge to the north of Loch Insh offers a slightly more ambitious starting point which adds three miles

The Bridge of Carr, Carrbridge. This wonderful span was built ►
in 1717 for £100 sterling.

▲ *En route to Loch Einich.*

(9.6km) to this route. Turn off at 844073 and follow a winding route past Alvie Lodge to join a track that follows the Allt na Cornlaraich to the Stag Hut, then continue north-west over Carn an Fhuarain Duibh to descend to the River Dulnain which is followed north-east to the point where you can join the track from Lynwilg.

Walk 22 Coylumbridge to Loch Einich and Braeriach
OS 36: 915108 circular
8 miles (5km) with 330ft (100m) of ascent

This route combines a gentle walk to a remote and beautiful loch with a return across the tops which is for experienced hill walkers and only to be attempted by them in good summer weather conditions. If you are saving your energies for the mountains, it may be a good idea to hire a bicycle at Aviemore for quicker access to the road-end at Loch Einich, even though this confines you to returning by the same route.

The Loch Einich path from the 'high road'. ▶

▲ *Higher up the path to Loch Einich. At one time this valley was densely forested.*

Start from Coylumbridge by following the more easterly of the two endings to Walk 20 in reverse. Pass Whitewell, but now leave Creag Dhubh to your right and continue south down the Gleann Einich path, which is signposted. The burn which crosses the road two miles (3.2km) short of the loch is impassable in spate. Loch Einich, which means Loch of the Marsh Glen, is a remote place crowded in with a cirque of mountains. Until quite recently remnants of the logging dam could be seen where the river emerges from the loch. Water would be released to float logs down to the Spey, and the roots of the felled Caledonian pines can still be seen in the boggy ground immediately below the loch.

To ascend Braeriach take the Coire Dhondail path, which branches left uphill just short of the loch and leads into the corrie, a recess between Braeriach and Creag an Loch. The path zigzags up Coire Dhondail to gain the flat ground above at 3232ft (985m). Now continue north more easily to the Wells of Dee (or take in Carn na Criche 4149ft (1265m) at the south edge of the Braeriach plateau).

▼ *Loch Einich. On the left is where the sluice gates controlled water for floating logs down to the Spey. On the hillside beyond the track to Braeriach slants up from left to right into Coire Dhondail, centre of photograph.*

The source of the River Dee is marked by a quartz cairn. At this altitude it erupts into the world as a powerful stream, and is unique in Britain in starting at 4000ft (1219m). After flowing a short way through gravelly banks it plunges 480ft (146m) over the cliffs of Garbh Choire Dhaidh into this 'rough corrie' below on its way down to Glen Dee. At the top of the Falls of Dee, even in spring, there is often a large snowbridge. The cliff scenery and the feeling of space makes the Braeriach plateau a really worthwhile outing. From the falls the crags continue and you should follow the edge round to rise to Braeriach (4248ft/1294m) above Coire Bhrochain, the Corrie of the Gruel.

If you don't now have to retrace your steps to recover your bike, it is possible to descend to the Lairig Ghru by going down to the col between Braeriach and Sron na Lairige. From here the Duke's Path descends the steep grass of Coire na Lairige to join the Lairig Ghru track close to the Pools of Dee, and the way back through

---

▼ *Coire Bhrochain in winter.*

▲ *Near the last of the pines on the ascent into the Lairig Ghru from Rothiemurchus.*

Rothiemurchus Forest to Coylumbridge. The Lairig Ghru is one of the most famous walks in Britain and deserves the separate attention which we shall give it now in Walk 23.

Walk 23   The Spey to the Dee by the Lairig Ghru
OS 36, 43: 915108 to 062896
18 miles (28km) with 2200ft (670m) of ascent

This pass through the Cairngorms from Rothiemurchus to Deeside is possibly the finest walk in Britain. It lifts you from the serene beauty of the Caledonian pines into a great glacial corridor, hemmed in by some of the highest

▲ *Early spring in the Lairig Ghru.*

mountains in the country. Austere and bleak though it may be at its highest point, it is also magnificent. In the days when the Lairig Ghru path was kept in good repair parties of Rothiemurchus women used to walk along it carrying baskets of fresh eggs on their heads to sell in Braemar. But do not be lulled into false confidence, it is a physically demanding walk on the finest of days and can become a serious expedition should the weather turn bad.

At 915108, close to Coylumbridge, take the rough road through the forest to the Cairngorm Club footbridge. Beyond the footbridge you arrive at a junction of four paths. Ahead the path leads to Loch Morlich, left from this junction the track goes to the old Medicine Well and the bridge over the River Luineag. The Lairig Ghru path

The Lairig Ghru from near Coylumbridge.　　　　　　　　　▲

The Cairngorm Club footbridge over the Allt Mor at the north end of the Lairig Ghru.　　　　　　　　　►

turns right, then climbs through the forest with superb views of tree, valley and mountain. Just over a mile further on a trail from Rothiemurchus Lodge and Glen More comes in from the left before you climb to the Sinclair Memorial Hut. Here the Lairig becomes more confined and stark. On the right is Sron na Lairige, on the left are the cliffs of Creag an Leth-choin. This is a windy place with violent gusts funnelling through the gap. Creag an Leth-choin, the Rock of the Lurcher, commemorates a great deer drive from Ryvoan, east of Glenmore Lodge, to Creag an Leth-choin where a lurcher fell to its death.

The summit of the Lairig Ghru is at 2738ft (835m). At one time the path was kept clear of stones, but not any more, and the going can be rough. This is a favourite haunt for ptarmigan. Just beyond the summit the March Burn, Allt na Criche, leaps down from the plateau to burrow underground. It reappears again as the Pools of Dee, one large and three small, on the Dee side of the summit. If you are patient you can see trout in the clear water. To the right is Braeriach with its stupendous

▼ *Looking down on the Pools of Dee from near the March Burn.*

▲ *Walkers approaching the Pools of Dee.*

▲ *The stream from the Pools of Dee goes underground for a short way before reappearing. The water drains south into the infant Dee.*

▲ *Braeriach, showing the Duke's Path, right of summit, which runs down into Coire na Lairige on the left to a point just south of the Pools of Dee.*

corries and the Duke's Path offering summer walking access to its summit from the Lairig Ghru and described as a descent route in Walk 22. The first of Braeriach's corries to reveal itself is An Garbh Choire, the Rough Corrie, a wonderfully isolated place. Immediately to the south of Braeriach's top is Coire Bhrochain, or Corrie of the Gruel. Ahead now is the summit of Cairn Toul and, behind but lower, Bod an Diabhail, a polite translation of which is Devil's Point.

Below Devil's Point a footbridge crosses the Dee to the Corrour Bothy and above on the left are the enormous screes of Ben Macdui. Opposite Corrour Bothy is a group of ribbed stones known as Clach nan Taillear, the Tailors' Stones, after a party of tailors who for a bet attempted to dance during a full winter's day at the three dells –

the Dell of Abernethy, the Dell of Rothiemurchus, and Dalnore in Mar. They traversed the Lairig to descend to Glen Dee when a blizzard struck. Clach nan Taillear was their last refuge place on this earth. Just past the Corrour Bothy junction the path divides and you can take either route. The right-hand fork leads down to White Bridge, passing en route Ciste Dhe, the Chest of Dee, a place of dark pools, rapids and square-topped rock scenery, well worth pausing to inspect. A further three miles (5km) will bring you to the road-end at the Linn of Dee. Overall, however, the left-hand branch has more to offer. It ascends to 2000ft (610m) to contour Sron Carn a' Mhaim and then runs east to Derry Lodge. This is a place of deer, pines and mountains with a Land Rover road running down to join the public road close to the Linn of Dee seven miles (11km) short of Braemar.

▼ *Looking north along the Lairig Ghru from high up the March Burn, with Aviemore in the distance.*

▲ *Looking to the south down the Lairig Ghru from the March Burn.*

▲ *The Lairig Ghru path snaking towards Rothiemurchus.*

▲ *The Lairig Ghru path above Derry Lodge.*

▲ *The alternative route to Braemar from the Lairig Ghru joins the Glen Tilt track here at White Bridge.*

▲ *Luibeg, last outpost on the Dee side of the Lairig Ghru.*

▲ *The Linn of Dee.*

▲ *The paths diverge: the Lairig Ghru and the Lairig an Laoigh and Braemar via Glen Lui.*

▲ *The Derry area has a large red deer population.*

Loch Morlich and Glen More Forest

Loch Morlich is the largest of the Speyside lochs, not very deep, but at a height of 1098ft (335m) it is never exactly warm for bathing in. The Glen More side is supposed to be haunted by a spirit who according to one seventeenth-century account "appears with a red hand in the habit of a Souldier and challenges men to fight with him . . . he fought with three Brothers, one after another, who immediately dyed thereafter".

The road which runs alongside the north shore of the loch offers superb views of the northern corries of the Cairngorms. Close to the camp-site it divides, one branch heading up to the ski complexes of the White Lady Shieling and Coire na Ciste, the other past the Scottish Sports Council's National Outdoor Training Centre at Glenmore Lodge to a gate. Here one can start various walks, all rewarding.

Walk 24   Glenmore, Meall a' Bhuachaille and Craiggowrie

OS 36: 988095 circular or to 934153
9 miles (14km) with 2000ft (609m) of ascent

First let us continue up this forest road a short stretch to An Lochan Uaine, the Green Loch. This lochan's total lack of vegetation, together with the minute flakes of mica in the water, allows the colour of its rocky bed to be reflected. Though sometimes close to the shore it can resemble custard, due to an accumulation of pollen. According to legend the water of Lochan Uaine derived its translucence from the fairies washing their clothes in it. One must speculate if it was from here that the well-known brand of washing-up liquid also obtained its name. In true fairy tradition there is an excellent echo from the loch.

◀ *Loch Morlich and Coire an t-Sneachda.*

▲ *An Lochan Uaine, the Green Loch. Ryvoan is at the low point on the ridge.*

Beyond An Lochan Uaine the left fork in the track leads to Ryvoan Bothy which over the years has become almost a shrine for hill walkers. The following anonymous verse was found there, poignantly, during the second world war:

I shall leave tonight from Euston
By the seven-thirty train,
And from Perth in the early morning
I shall see the hills again.
From the top of Ben Macdhui
I shall watch the gathering storm.
And see the crisp snow lying
At the back of Cairngorm.
I shall feel the mist from Bhrotain
And pass by the Lairig Ghru
To look on dark Loch Einich
From the heights of Sgoran Dubh.
From the broken Barns of Bynack
I shall see the sunrise gleam
On the forehead of Ben Rinnes,
And Strathspey awake from dream.
And again in the dusk of evening
I shall find once more alone
The dark waters of the Green Loch.
And the pass beyond Revoan.
For tonight I leave from Euston
And leave the world behind.
Who has the hills as a lover
Will find them wondrous kind.

Beyond Ryvoan the track continues to Nethy Bridge via Rynettin and Forest Lodge, a distance of ten miles (16km). However, to capture stunning views of the area, if the weather is kind, take the track leading north-west from Ryvoan up to the summit of Meall a' Bhuachaille (2654ft/808m). Continue to Creagan Gorm (2403ft/732m). From the col between the two the path striking off left takes you back down to Glenmore. But if the weather holds and the spirit is willing, continue along the

▲ *Ryvoan Bothy looking towards the Lairig an Laoigh.*

ridge. The route provides easy going and encounters a huge erratic of pink granite before the next unnamed peak. The final summit is Craiggowrie (2237ft/681m). Now a well demarked path leads down to the old settlement of Badaguish, where various forest roads lead back to Loch Morlich.

As an alternative to returning to Loch Morlich it is possible to continue south-west along a minor forestry track and then turn right along the forest road running north-west by the pass of An Slugan, the Gullet, which is part of an old right of way and takes one to the B970 north of Loch Pityoulish. Of course this route can also be used for a short but pleasant excursion from Loch Morlich to Loch Pityoulish.

Walk 25   Glenmore to Cairngorm
OS 36: 976099 circular
4.5 miles (7km) to Cairngorm summit with 2944ft (897m) of ascent

Cairngorm (4083ft/1245m), the Blue Hill, is nowadays synonymous with winter sport. It was here in 1961 that skiing became big business in the Highlands with the advent of the access road into Coire Cas and the subsequent chairlifts. Though many feel that this area has been spoiled for the discerning walker, others accept it as part and parcel of increased leisure time and recreation. Non-skiers can certainly make use of the chairlifts to gain quick access to the plateau and thereby engage in walks which would otherwise be beyond their capabilities. With this facility, however, comes the possible danger of being caught out on this exposed plateau without the physical ability to return to a lower and safer altitude should the weather break.

From Glenmore camp-site it is possible to take the old path up Cairngorm part of the way at least. You can pick it up from the access road by the Allt Mor just beyond the bridge halfway up the forest. Above it crosses the road at the large bend and angles uphill beside the massive boulder called Clach Bharraig to the An t-Aonach ridge. Follow on up the long ridge of Sron an Aonaich, the Nose of the Height, bypassing the granite tor of Caisteal Dubh, to arrive at the Ptarmigan restaurant. From here it is less than a mile, and 480ft (146m) of ascent to the summit of Cairngorm.

▼ *The Ptarmigan restaurant close to the summit of Cairngorm.*

▲ *The summit of Cairngorm with its remote meteorological and mountain rescue repeater stations.*

▲ *The edge of the plateau and the cliffs and gullies of Coire an Lochain.*

▲ *The superb cliffs of Coire an Lochain.*

You can descend via Cairn Lochan which is a distance of 3.3 miles (5km), then on to Creag an Leth-choin. Go west from the summit of Cairngorm to Fiacaill a' Choire Chais (3742ft/1141m) where the path runs south down to a col before rising gently in a clockwise curve along the cliff edge of Coire an t-Sneachda, Corrie of the Snow. The highest point is 3857ft (1176m). Descend to another col, then up to the top of Coire Domhain, and after this a short climb takes you to the summit of Cairn Lochan (3985ft/1215m). From Cairngorm to this point it is 1.8 miles with 576ft (176m) of ascent. Both Coire an t-Sne-achda and Coire an Lochain are impressive places with wonderful rock architecture. The route now descends west to join a wide ridge. At the end of the flat section is a cairn, Carn nan Tri Crioch, Cairn of the Three Boundaries (981018). The best descent is directly down the wide

ridge that begins at the north end of the grassy area. This is called the Fiachaill an Leth-choin and links up with the path which skirts the base of the corries back to Coire Cas car park, or alternatively, you can join the Glenmore path via the footbridge over the Allt Mor which is just to the south of the trees. From Cairn Lochan by Fiachaill an Leth-choin to the car park is three miles (5km).

Walk 26   Cairngorm summit to Ryvoan
OS 36: 005040 to 005115
5 miles (8km)

This is an excellent route back to Glenmore from the top of Cairngorm. Go down the north ridge to Cnap Coire na Spreidhe, Knob of the Cattle Corrie (3772ft/1149m), bypassing the cliffs, with good views of Strath Nethy to the right. Continue on beyond the 3374ft (1028m) top to descend the nose of Sron a' Cha-no to Lochan na Beinne. A path on the west side of the loch leads north-west to the Ryvoan road. The distance is five miles (8km) from the summit of Cairngorm.

◄ *The Coire an Lochain slab avalanche which comes down every spring. It can be massive.*

▼ *Looking east from Cairngorm summit.*

▲ *Picking out landmarks to the south from the summit of Cairngorm.*

Alternatively, instead of descending to the loch, you can continue on to Stac na h-Iolaire to descend to Mam Suim and Creag na Gall above An Lochan Uaine. This route allows you to view valleys which were cut by huge rivers outflowing from the enormous Glen More glacier 10,000 years ago. Stac na h-Iolaire, Eagle's Corrie, and Eag a' Gharbh Choire are of particular interest.

Walk 27   Glenmore to Ben Macdui by Cairngorm
OS 36: 976099 to 989989
4 miles (6.5km) with 880ft (268m) of ascent

Ben Macdui (4293ft/1309m) despite its remoteness is one of the most popular hill walks in the Cairngorms and is the second highest mountain in the British Isles. Its popularity is well justified, for it is surrounded with wonderful scenery, tarns and precipices on a grand scale and it is the most arctic-like area in the country. The name probably means Macduff's hill, or the hill of the sons of Duff.

Nowadays, with the advent of the chairlift up Cairngorm, this approach is by far the most common line of ascent. So one cannot repeat too often the warning about attempting the traverse of the high plateau ill-equipped even in midsummer.

The route from Cairngorm is as described in Walk 25 for Cairn Lochan. From the col to the east of this peak at 3648ft (1111m), which is at the edge of the Coire an t-Sneachda cliffs, a small path angles uphill along the west side of Coire Domhain in a south-westerly direction before levelling out and continuing to Lochan Buidhe, the Yellow Tarn, known in earlier times as Lochan Feidh Buidhe, the highest named tarn in Britain. Its waters flow down into Banffshire, though just a short way west, beyond the turfy ground, water also drains into the Allt na Criche, the March Burn.

It was in the general area round this lochan that many cairngorm crystals were found in the past. An old woman

▲ *Cairngorm top left, with the edge of Coire an t-Sneachda leading towards the camera.*

▲ *Coire an t-Sneachda in winter.*

▲ *The head of Coire an t-Sneachda in winter.*

▲ *A view east from near Lochan Buidhe, showing Loch Avon with Shelter Stone Crag on the right. Cairngorm is out of picture left.*

who went under the name of Cailleach nan Clach, the Old Woman of the Stones, spent part of her life up here in search of cairngorms and found many of considerable value. Asked if she was ever frightened, spending lonely days and even nights in this remote place with its reputation of ghosts and spectres, she replied that she never saw anything worse than her own reflection in the clear pools. Another cairngorm hunter was James Grant, who lived at Ryvoan. Beside the Feith Bhuidhe he found a fifty-pound (22kg) crystal which Queen Victoria bought for the princely sum of £50. There are tales, too, of a large crystal which hunters of both deer and crystals have reputedly seen from the Shelter Stone at the head of Loch Avon (Loch A'an) sparkling by moonlight on a cliff to the north side of the loch. But it has never been found.

Past Lochan Buidhe cairns indicate the way southwards to the summit of Ben Macdui's north top, then on south-south-west across the flat summit to the cairn. The summit is reputed to be haunted by Liath Mor, the Big Grey Man. The late Professor Norman Collie, a great Victorian pioneer of climbing and a former President of the Alpine Club, had a frightening encounter close to the summit when he heard a distinct crunching of giant feet in the snow which then followed him with fearful persistence across the plateau. Many others have felt an ominous presence on the summit of this mountain, and as recently as the 1940s an Aberdeen climber emptied his army revolver into a menacing spectre which appeared in the mist. There are tales, too, that the grass growing on this high place was poisonous to horses due to glutinous matter ejected by the Famh, a legendary monster which showed itself only at dawn at the head of Loch Avon. This does

A stony wilderness. The summit of Ben Macdui and not a Big Grey Man in sight. ►

Lochan Buidhe, between Cairngorm and Ben Macdui. It was close to here that a huge cairngorm was found. ► ►

▲ *The cliffs of Creagan a' Choire Etchachan in summer, a mecca for rock climbers. The Shelter Stone track is seen bottom right.*

not appear to have put off Queen Victoria, however, who ascended Ben Macdui on a pony in 1859, only one of her many Cairngorm feats. She wrote of her expedition thus: "Never shall I forget this day, or the impression this very grand scene made upon me; truly sublime and impressive; such solitude."

Walk 28   Glen Derry to Ben Macdui
OS 36: 040934 to 989989
7.5 miles (12km) with 2900ft (883m) of ascent

Starting from Derry Lodge on the track north up Glen Derry, the climb is gradual and very fine indeed. It is the path for the Lairig an Laoigh. At 035992 follow the signpost left to the north-west to cross the Etchachan Burn via a footbridge and gain Coire Etchachan and the lonely Hutchison Hut at 2296ft (700m). Coire Etchachan is an impressive place and as if by magic you arrive at

Coire Etchachan and the crags of Creagan a' Choire Etchachan. ▲
The routes to Ben Macdui and the Shelter Stone branch off from here.

A view south-east from above the head of Loch Avon towards ▶
Creagan a' Choire Etchachan which is beyond the line of figures.

Loch Etchachan. This loch usually has ice in it for more than half the year and is the highest loch of its size in Britain. Northwards over a level col is a route to Loch Avon (see Walk 29) with Cairngorm beyond. Beware in taking compass bearings, as there is some magnetic rock in the area. To the left is Carn Etchachan. From the east end of the loch the Ben Macdui trail angles up left to beneath the snout of Sron an Daimh, the Nose of the Stag, to emerge on the lip of the basin close to a cliff top on the left-hand side. This cliff forms the edge of Coire Sputan Dearg, the Corrie with Little Red Spouts, from the red scree in the principal gullies. The path now climbs by the cliff edge with superb views to the plateau. Go west over the gravelly terrain past a ruined bothy to the summit of Ben Macdui. The bothy was used in the nineteenth century by sappers engaged in the survey of the Cairngorms.

Descend from the summit by the route to Cairn Lochan and just before Lochan Buidhe slant left where the path follows the edge of the Lairig Ghru. This takes you to the descent route for Walk 25 down the Fiachaill an Leth-choin in a northerly direction to meet up with the path leading round to the Cairngorm road.

Loch Avon is a superb sweep of water in a deep mountain trench at 2374ft (723m) in the most inaccessible heart of the Cairngorms. It is well worth a visit for those with determination and energy and can be approached from the south and the north. It is not advisable to attempt either approach in winter or when snow is lying, for in the event of bad weather it can be difficult to return fast to civilisation.

▲ *The Fiacaill Ridge and Coire Lochain to the right.*

◄ *Reindeer in the northern Cairngorms.*

▲ *Looking down on the turfy area at the head of Loch Avon called Meur na Banaraiche, the Finger of the Dairymaid.*

◄ *The head of Loch Avon with Creagan a' Choire Etchachan top right.*

Walk 29   Glen Derry to Loch Avon by Loch Etchachan

OS 36: 040934 to 002015
7 miles (11km) with 1640ft (502m) of ascent

From Derry Lodge follow the Ben Macdui Walk 28 as far as Loch Etchachan. The route then crosses flat ground to the north of the loch to descend steeply to the Shelter Stone, Clach Dhion. The view into Loch Avon is dramatic and the descent from Loch Etchachan equally so, yet easy enough on a path traversing beneath the rocky bastion of the north spur of Carn Etchachan. The Shelter Stone is easily identified by the cairn on its top. In the eighteenth century it was a freebooters' hideout capable of holding

---

Shelter Stone Crag from the east close to the path to Derry Lodge ►
via Loch Etchachan.

Carn Etchachan and Shelter Stone Crag with Creagan a' ► ►
Choire Etchachan top left.

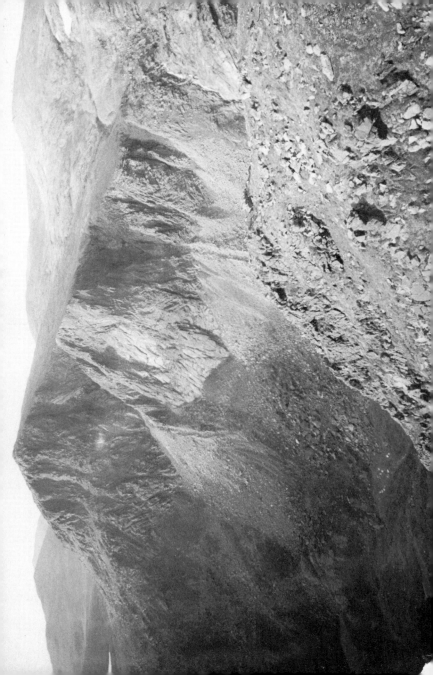

▲ *Cairngorm and Loch Avon. At the bottom left of the loch is the way to the Lairig an Laoigh with the Saddle visible. The easier slope up left from the patch of ice-free water is an access route from the plateau in summer. This photograph was taken in April.*

'eighteen armed men'. Today its function is much the same, but its habitués are rock climbers and winter mountaineers who have made this famous doss quite snug with turf and drystone walling. The oldest climbing club in Scotland, the Cairngorm Club, was founded here on 24th June, 1887, the morning after Queen Victoria's Golden Jubilee, and ever since 1924 there has been a visitors' book under the stone.

Walk 30   Bynack Stable to Loch Avon by Strath Nethy and the Saddle

OS 36: 020105 to 002018
6 miles (10km) with 1508ft (460m) of ascent from Glenmore

Bynack Stable is just over a mile south-east of Ryvoan Bothy. After crossing the River Nethy going east, take the right-hand fork where the track divides and follow it south to the Saddle at 2646ft (804m). For walkers with

---

◀ *The Shelter Stone is the large boulder marked X. The cairn on the front edge gives an idea of scale.*

▲ *Looking across the top of Shelter Stone Crag on to the headwall of Loch Avon.*

---

limited experience this is the safest approach. From the Saddle take the path up the north side of the loch to the Shelter Stone. Ahead is some of the finest rock architecture in the Cairngorms, with the headwall rising in spectacular grandeur and white ribbons of water uniting in one stream, the Garbh Uisge, the Rough Water, which cascades through a green patch of turf and flowers called Meur na Banaraiche, the Finger of the Dairymaid, before entering the loch.

It is also possible to reach Loch Avon from the Lairig an Laoigh path which joins the Strath Nethy track at Bynack Stable. On this longer approach, cut west along the true left bank of the Avon at 043032 and follow the path along the south side of the loch. For more detail on the Lairig an Laoigh see Walk 62.

Walk 31 Cairngorm summit to the Shelter Stone
OS 36: 005040 to 002015
2.8 miles (4.5km)

An easier route to Loch Avon comes in from the north, if you take the Cairngorm chairlift and descend carefully to the head of the loch by the Allt Coire Raibeirt on a path descending the easier eastern side of the steep section of the burn.

The B970 continues north along the east side of the Spey beyond Aviemore. At Loch Pityoulish there once lived a waterhorse which is reported to have shown itself "gaily caparisoned, with saddle and bridle, bright with silver and gems" to lure the innocent into the bowels of the loch. Nearby Lag-nan-Ciumeanach, the Hollow of the Cummings, is reputed to smell of blood ever since one Shaw Mackintosh, with members of his clan, killed a party of Cummings here. It was also in this loch that Colonel Thornton, a pioneer Highland sportsman, caught an enormous pike, weighing forty-eight pounds (21kg) and measuring five feet four inches long (1.6m).

Further along the B970 on the right towards Boat of Garten and Nethy Bridge stands the Church of Kincardine (938156) which dates from the fifteenth century, and

▼ *The Church of Kincardine. Note the small leper window to the right of the chimney.*

is the scene of another massacre of the hapless Cummings who took refuge in the church. But the avenging Stewarts and Grants fired the thatch and all the Cummings inside perished save one man of great stature who fought manfully, though blinded by smoke and rage, until he was finally slain on the doorstep.

Across the Spey the privately-owned Strathspey Railway Company runs steam trains at regular intervals during the tourist season from Aviemore to Boat of Garten. Boat refers to the fact that there was a ferry here until the bridge was built in 1899. Further along the road is the right turnoff for Loch Garten, a peaceful spot in the Abernethy pine forest and famous in recent years as a place for osprey-spotting under the careful auspices of the Royal Society for the Protection of Birds. This is a region abounding in forest walks and a glance at the map will reveal many Hansel and Gretel excursions, for it is an area in which to get pleasantly lost.

▼ *Steam trains run between Aviemore and Boat of Garten in the tourist season. Inset, an inducement to travel.*

▲ *Castle Roy, just to the north of Nethy Bridge, over seven centuries old. There is a tradition that treasure infected by plague lies within the walls.*

Nethy Bridge is the start or finish of the long Lairig an Laoigh trek via Ryvoan and Bynack which we shall approach later from the opposite end in Walk 62. Here the York Buildings Company of London set up a charcoal furnace and iron ore used to be transported over the Lecht on strings of pack ponies. The attendant prosperity caused the local minister to fulminate: "Their extravagances of every kind ruined themselves and corrupted others. They used to display their vanity by bonfires, tar barrels and opening hogsheads of brandy to the country people, by which five of them died in one night." At nearby Lynstock there used to be a gallows tree and at one particular lynching two brothers were hanged together and buried at the base of it.

Castle Roy is close to the B970 just over a mile on the Grantown side of Nethy Bridge. It is probably one of the earliest fortalices in the country and one of the most basic in design, dating from the thirteenth century.

Walk 32 Nethy Bridge to Tomintoul
OS 36: 003207 to 168187
14 miles (22.5m)

Take the Tomintoul road east from Nethy Bridge for three miles (4.8km) and turn right at the fork which leads to Dorback Lodge. Go round the Lodge to the left and on to Fae, then Letteraitten, and by an old road leading east to the Burn of Brown (cross at the ford). On the other bank a path continues down the east side of the burn until it connects with a forest road which climbs, still in an easterly direction, beyond Stronachavie to meet up with the Grantown–Tomintoul A939 a short way above the Bridge of Avon. From here it is one and a half miles to Tomintoul.

Dulnain Bridge is at the junction of the A95 and the A938 and the river of that name joins forces with the Spey a short way to the south-east. The ancient name for the valley of Dulnain was the Valley of the Freebooter. Poaching too has a long local history. An early reference

---

◄ *The road to Tomintoul.*

▼ *Dulnain Bridge, the old Spey bridge of 1754 close to Grantown.*

▲ *Castle Grant, Grantown. Queen Victoria thought it resembled a factory.*

to the River Dulnain mentions, "There comes no salmon in this water, but extraordinary much Kipper, that is salmon in the forbidden time which are in such abundance, that a gentleman thinks nothing to kill 160 a night. They used to feast the Sheriff, and so escape the fine, but the Commonality pay some little thing."

Grantown-on-Spey

Grantown-on-Spey dates only from the latter half of the eighteenth century and like Kingussie was more or less custom built for the Laird of Grant. The railway arrived in 1863. King Edward VII was a visitor and both he and the Kaiser bought their tweeds in the town. There are many fine walks in the district, especially those by the riverside. A mile out of town to the north, close to the A939, is Castle Grant. The fine gatehouse was built by the Highland Railway Company in gratitude for permission to construct their now defunct railway across

◀ *The old private railway station of Castle Grant.*

Grant land. Queen Victoria summed up the pile well when she called it a "very plain looking house, like a factory". However, it was John Adam who had redesigned the north front and it does have an interesting history. Originally it was the Castle of Freuchie, an L-shaped tower house of the fifteenth century, before being transformed into the lofty mansion about which Queen Victoria was so disparaging. A rather macabre relic dated from the time when it had been a Comyn stronghold. A Grant known as 'Hard Ian' killed an incumbent Comyn and the dead man's skull was preserved, cut in two and hinged – a snuff-box, perhaps?

Just east of Grantown the A95 runs through Cromdale, and nearby to the south-east is the site of the Battle of Cromdale, the last organised resistance to Williamite rule, which was fought in 1690, a year after Killiecrankie. Here, Colonel Sir Thomas Livingstone, King William's general, faced the remnants of Claverhouse's force of Highlanders, commanded by General Buchan. Despite a valiant fight, the Highlanders were defeated with 300 of their 800 troops slain. The battle is commemorated in the song:

> I met a man in tartan trews,
> I speired [asked] at him what was the news;
> Quoth he, "The Highland army rues
> That ere they cam tae Cromdale."

To the south of the village, up the hill, is the Balmenach Distillery which started its life as an illicit still and became one of the first licensed distilleries on Speyside.

Between Cromdale and the junction with the A939 there is a large interesting cairn circle in a field south of Congash Farm. There are also several Pictish symbol stones, one with a double disc and Z-rod. It is unfortunate that such an historic site is so neglected.

Lochindorb Castle to the north of Grantown, a stronghold of the ▶
Wolf of Badenoch.

Walk 33 Cromdale to Bridge of Brown

OS 36: 075285 to 124206
6 miles (10km) with 1696ft (516m) of ascent

Take the road south up to Lethendry Castle, where some of the defeated Highlanders hid after the Battle of Cromdale. Now take the track to the east skirting a plantation close to the site of the battle. Go up the slope to a col south-west of Creagan a' Chaise (2368ft/722m), which is the highest point of the Hills of Cromdale. Then descend to Mains of Glenlochy to the south-east and Bridge of Brown on the A939 four miles from Tomintoul.

Tomintoul
Tomintoul gives the impression that it has been placed high in the middle of nowhere as an architectural practical joke. It was in fact founded by the fourth Duke of Gordon in 1750 and laid out in somewhat stern geometrical lines. It was also on General Wade's military road and by 1860, when that much travelled Queen, Victoria, visited it, she was not impressed: "the most tumble-down poor looking place I ever saw – a long street with three inns, miserable, dirty-looking houses and people, and a sad look of wretchedness about it". Today Tomintoul is a super village – in summertime – and enjoys a healthy tourist trade, with the famous Glenlivet Distillery within staggering distance. Many visitors are under the impression that Tomintoul is the highest village in Scotland, but this is not the case. (Wanlockhead in Dumfriesshire holds this record.) But Tomintoul must have the distinction of being Scotland's most mentioned village in weather reports, for it is frequently cut off and the Lecht Road, which (usually) connects it with Cock Bridge to the south-east, is often impassable in winter.

There is an interesting walk to Tomintoul from Strathdon but, before you march off out of the Strathdon area, find time to visit Kildrummy Castle.

Kildrummy Castle

This outstanding relic of Scottish history is a short distance north of Strathdon on the A97 towards Huntly. On the way you will pass the roofless ruin of Glenbuchat Castle, built on the Z-plan in the late sixteenth century. Over the entrance is the inscription: *Nothing on arth remains bot fame. John Gordon-Helen Carnagie 1590.* The Gordons were ardent supporters of Bonnie Prince Charlie and one was the Prince's brigadier-general in both the '15 and '45 Risings.

Kildrummy Castle is a vast pile dating from the thirteenth century and used to be one of the greatest castles in Scotland. It was here that Bruce's brother, Nigel, was betrayed to the English by the castle blacksmith and captured, together with the Queen, the Princess and his sisters. Later the son of the Wolf of Badenoch took the castle and forced the Mar heiress to marry him. The first

▼ *Kildrummy Castle with the large defence ditch in the foreground.*

Lord Elphinstone obtained the castle in 1507 and the family managed to hold on to it until 1626 when the Erskine Earls of Mar got it back. In 1654 the Royalists set up a garrison here, but it fell to Cromwell's supporters. It was finally dismantled after the Rising of 1715 and the castle is now a ruin, but an imposing one. It is said that a vaulted tunnel which led from the castle to Burnside was high enough to accommodate a mounted horse. Both Kildrummy and Glenbuchat are now under the care of the Department of the Environment.

Walk 34   Strathdon to Tomintoul by the Ladder Hills and Glen Livet

OS 37, 36: 355131 to 177191
18 miles (28km) with 1408ft (429m) of ascent

This is an interesting approach to Tomintoul. From Strathdon take the road leading up the Water of Nochty from Strathdon and fork left to Auchernach and Alda-chuie. Go through a gate leading into Forestry Commission land some 200 yards (62m) beyond and follow the track which crosses the burn to Duffdefiance and carries on north-west to the Ladder Hills. Duffdefiance got its name from a crofter who came over the Ladder from Glen Livet and built himself a house without permission. He had the 'lum reekin' – the chimney smoking – before the local Duff laird arrived on the scene and so, according to Highland tradition, he could not be thrown out and his house received its name.

Beyond Duffdefiance you ascend by a bulldozed road to arrive at a plateau and when the road runs out a path takes over; take this to the summit at 2410ft (735m), close to a cairn. On the other side the path, sometimes difficult to follow, descends by the Ladder Burn to the Braes of

▲ *Harvest time in Mar.*

◄ *Craigievar Castle.*

▲ *At the crossroads in Strathdon, the start of the Ladder Hills walk.*

Glenlivet, now almost a ghost village. Continue on from Chapeltown to Lettoch, then south-west over the hill, through a plantation, to gain the Tomintoul–Dufftown road beside Inchnacape Farm about two and a half miles (4km) from Tomintoul. If you decide to do this route in reverse take care when you reach the Forestry Commission land beyond Duffdefiance to locate the public path leading to Aldachuie.

Walk 35   Tomintoul to Cabrach by the Steplar
OS 36, 37: 177191 to 387268
17 miles (27km)

The Steplar is an ancient right of way and former drove road. Start where Walk 34 ended, some two and a half miles (4km) along the B9008 Dufftown road from Tomintoul. Go through the gate 150 yards (46m) past Inchnacape Farm entrance and climb over the hill through Forestry Commission ground to Lettoch, Clashnoir and Burnside of Thain. A track from here goes north-east over to the River Livet to meet up with a rough road which runs to the ruins of Suie. Past Suie the road continues north, but bear right after about 200 yards (62m) at 278252 and take the old cart road to join up with a better road two miles (3.2km) on which runs east to the ford at the Black Water. Beyond this, close to the deer fence by the Dead Wife's Hillock, the path is somewhat indistinct but a rough road lying to the east of the deer fence runs down to Aldivalloch. A proper highway now continues to Cabrach. The name Cabrach means plentiful in tree poles or cabers.

Walk 36   Tomintoul to Crathie
OS 36, 37: 174188 to 265950
22 miles (35km) with 2800ft (853m) of ascent

This walk through to Deeside follows an old drove road for the first part of the way and then a 1750s military road.

Start from Blairnamarrow on the Lecht Road (A939) some three and a half miles (5.6km) to the south-east of Tomintoul. Go south over the hill between the peaks of Tolm Buirich and Carn Ealasaid to Dunanfiew. From here, head east along the Don for two miles (3.2km) to Cock Bridge. Half a mile down the A939 to the right, turn off on a road to the right for Ordgarff and where this forks take the right-hand one south over Carn Mor and Tom Odhar along a section of drove road called the Camus Road. After Easter Sleach cross the River Gairn and follow up its true left bank for one and a half miles before taking a track south-east to Blairglass, and on down to join the B976 close to Bush Lawsie and Crathie, with Balmoral Castle across the Dee.

Walk 37   Tomintoul to Cock Bridge by Avon and Don
OS 36, 37: 171184 to 258090
14 miles (22km)

From the southern outskirts of Tomintoul, take the estate road which winds south up the east bank of the River Avon to Inchrory. This is a superb section along a renowned salmon river, with water cascading through rocky defiles. At Inchrory take the road to the left which curves east round Cairn Culchavie to join a road along the south side of the Don at Delnadamph Lodge all the way to Cock Bridge.

Just to the south of Cock Bridge stands the stark structure of Corgarff Castle which seems to symbolise remoteness and solitude. It was burned in 1571 when, on the orders of Gordon of Auchinduin, a Captain Ker burned alive Lady Forbes, together with her children and servants, twenty-seven in all. (This tale is also told of Towie Castle which has been demolished.) Later Corgarff Castle passed back to the Earldom of Mar, then to the Forbeses. In 1689 it was burned by the Jacobites and the government emulated this deed in 1716, certain flam-

▲ *Corgarff Castle, Cock Bridge.*

mable furnishings having presumably been reinstalled in the interim. One can only hope that the present occupants have it insured.

Walk 38   Cock Bridge to Nethy Bridge by Glen Avon and the Lairig an Laoigh
OS 37, 36: 258090 to 011200
32 miles (51km) with 1300ft (396m) of ascent

Inchrory, the halfway point of Walk 37, is the first pivot of this walk. You can approach it from Cock Bridge to the east, or from Tomintoul to the north. Just south of

Inchrory a Land Rover track runs along the River Avon which has made a big swing to the west. Eventually it dwindles to a path at Faindouran Bothy after making another major turn to the south-west. Continuing on you meet the Lairig an Laoigh track where it crosses the Avon at the Ford of the Fianna. From here you can follow a combination of Walks 30 and 26 to reach Glenmore Lodge, or the more energetic can follow the Lairig an Laoigh all the way north to Nethy Bridge. The Lairig an Laoigh is described in full in Walk 62.

The Valley of the Dee
The valley of the Dee's royal associations date from the time when Queen Victoria divided her year between Windsor, Osborne on the Isle of Wight, and Balmoral. It was Balmoral which was her favourite place and neighbouring Braemar and Ballater have thrived on the royal connection ever since. The valley of the Dee is also, as Queen Victoria indefatigably discovered for herself, an area abounding in marvellous walks.

In exploring Royal Deeside we shall start with some walks based on Ballater, then move east to take in some classic routes, before retracing our steps west to the royal haunts of Balmoral Forest, Loch Muick, Lochnagar and Braemar. But first, Ballater is an excellent starting-off point.

Ballater
Ballater is a pleasant, busy little town, laid out in sober lines, which gives one the impression that it has just been spring-cleaned. Like several other towns flanking the Cairngorms, it was planned from birth, in this case by the Farquharson laird in 1770. The mineral wells at Pannanich, a couple of miles (3.2km) to the south-east, were a fashionable attraction in the eighteenth century but I would guess that today the most popular drink at the Pannanich Wells Hotel is not the natural mineral water!

Just north of Ballater Craigendarroch, the Rock of the Oaks (1319ft/402m), is worth climbing, and there are some wonderful oaks on its lower reaches. The path zigzags upwards, and above it encircles the hill with two further paths leading to the top. Take the left path to the north end, then climb to the summit and descend the south-west side. The 'peaklet' is of granite and the top ice-smoothed bedrock. It boasts a fine view, though the path now suffers from erosion.

Behind Craigendarroch is the deep defile of the Pass of Ballater, through which runs the B972. A Farquharson stronghold used to guard the western end, but little remains today.

Another rock offering an even better panorama from its top rises abruptly above the Dee bridge. This projection, Craig Coillich, the Old Woman's Rock, gives a climb of 1270ft (387m). There is a path starting through the pines and this is the route taken by perspiring hill runners in Ballater's annual Highland Games.

Walk 39   Walk o' the Seven Brigs
OS 44: 374955 to 365960
5 miles (8km)

This short circular walk is a must if you are staying in Ballater. From Ballater Bridge (bridge one) take the road to Glen Muick and just past the estate entrance of the now defunct Glen Muick House, you cross the second bridge at the top of Spinning Jenny, called after a local witch. Continue along to where a burn meets the River Dee. Here is the third bridge. The road (B976) now goes off right and crosses the fourth bridge (circa 1872) over the River Muick. Close by on the left is an old graveyard in a lovely setting with many rough stones, one dated 1598. Pursuit of the fifth bridge takes you up the first opening on the right after the graveyard.

But Knock Castle just a little way further along on the

B976 is a worthwhile diversion. The tower of this Huntly stronghold dates from the early seventeenth century and is built on the site of an older structure. Shortly after its completion, the Forbeses attacked the Huntly sons who were peat cutting in the vicinity and dispatched them all to their ancestors. Upon receiving this dire news, their father fell down the castle stairs and broke his neck. Forbes of Strathgirnock hanged for the murders. The Scurry Stane, a standing stone, is close by.

To return to our walk, take the first opening on the right (north) after the graveyard and gain a gravel road to Polhollick where you cross the Dee once more by a white suspension bridge. Now head back towards Ballater on the main road to bag the next bridge which is over the River Gairn. Beyond it go right again and take a small path which goes down the 'Old Line', a railway which never was. The proposal was to link Aberdeen and Braemar by rail, but the line would have had to pass Balmoral, and that passionate Highlander, Queen Victoria, was not amused. Now comes the seventh and last bridge which spans the gorge called the 'Postie Leap'. Tradition has it that a local postman committed suicide here when he was jilted on the eve of his wedding.

Walk 40   Ballater to Morven
OS 37: 356969 to 377040
12 miles (19km) with 2250ft (685m) of ascent

Morven (2857ft/871m), to the north of Ballater, is easily climbed from the town. Go east along the Pass of Ballater road for a quarter of a mile and take the track up Creagan Riach. Go up the valley of the Tullich Burn (don't go west) to reach the ruins of an old lodge. Now it's grassy slopes to the top. You can also walk up from Tullich, just east of the bridge. Go first by a farm road then a good trail to the east of Crannach Hill. For the last section there is no path.

Walk 41   Ballater to Cock Bridge
OS 37: 354970 to 258092
12 miles (19km) with 984ft (300m) of ascent

From the Bridge of Gairn on the Braemar road, take the minor road on the right up the east bank of the Gairn to Lary. Here a path leads north-west up Glen Fenzie to the Glas Choille military road which is also the A939 and has to be endured for two and a half miles (4km) before you turn off to the left a mile after the high point at 298061. This path leads north-west again and crosses the Burn of Tornahaish to reach a big bend in the River Don. Take the south bank of the Don to the north-west for Cock Bridge.

Walk 42   Ballater to Strathdon
OS 37: 354970 to 355127
14 miles (22km) with 2156ft (657m) of ascent

Take the route of Walk 41 as far as Lary but this time follow the right-hand road towards but not to Morven Lodge. After one and a quarter miles take the rough road up right following the Morven Burn to the north-west of Morven and descend the col to the Deskry Water which leads you down to the Strathdon road (A97) at Boultenstone, where there is a pub. By taking the first turning off the A97 to the left you can approach Strathdon itself by pleasanter back roads and avoid the main road traffic.

There is a variation on this route for those wanting to return to the valley of the Dee. Some two miles (3km) north of Lary a track heads off east to traverse the southern slopes of Morven, then slants down to Barglass. From here carry on to the A97 at Homehead.

An even shorter diversion from this track is to return in a circular tour to Ballater by taking Walk 40 in reverse down the east side of Crannach Hill to Milton of Tullich.

The elegant 1751 bridge across the River Gairn near Ballater.   ▶
Inset, a warning on the Bridge of Gairn to Cock Bridge road.

Risk of
grounding
5 miles
ahead

Dinnet

Dinnet, just east of Ballater on the A93, is a pleasant village set among wonderful pines and the nearby Lochs Kinord and Kavan are both lovely and rich in history. At the east end of Loch Kinord there is a man-made island – a crannog, marked on the OS 44 but not on the OS 37. While to the west another small island houses a ruined fortification built, according to tradition, by Malcolm Canmore in the eleventh century and also used by James IV. It was taken by Covenanting forces in the seventeenth century and later dismantled.

On the land between the two lochs a Pictish village has been excavated, possibly Devana. There are several blue cairns some way to the east and a further clutch of cairns on Mulloch Hill which may have been connected with the village. A symbol stone of Pictish origin can still be viewed on a hillock between Old and New Kinord.

At the A97 roadside near the Vat Burn is a monolith commemorating the Battle of Culblean, the last battle of the second War of Independence fought in 1335, six years after Bruce's death. Another commemorative boulder is the Great Stane, which stands on the side of Culblean Hill, close to the Vat Burn. It was here that Atholl made his last stand. The Vat is a natural cauldron in the ravine of the Vat Burn formed in a twin cavern with a minuscule crevasse entrance in the rocks. This was the hideaway of a notorious MacGregor called Gilderoy, a seventeenth-century freebooter who gave the residents of Cromar many sleepless nights. There is access from the parking area at Burn o' Vat.

Two fine walks start from Dinnet and take you over two of the region's historic named roads, the Mounth Road and the Firmounth Road, both running north–south between the Dee and the Esk valleys. Mounth, aptly enough, means mountain.

◄ *The last section of the Bridge of Gairn-Cock Bridge route from the A939.*

Walk 43 Dinnet to Glen Esk by Glen Tanar and the Mounth

OS 44: 467983 to 445804
13 miles (22km)

Cross the Dee from Dinnet and turn left along the B976 for a quarter of a mile, then turn right to Tillycairn where there is a stone to commemorate, probably erroneously, the passage this way of Edward I in 1296. (It is more likely his peregrinations took him across either the Fungle or the Cryne Corse Mounth further to the east.) Cross Tillyburn and continue south-east over Belrorie Hill to the quaint old bridge over the Water of Tanar at Millfield. Cross the bridge and walk south along the river opposite Glen Tanar House, recrossing below the house at the Bridge of Knockie. The road up Glen Tanar now runs to the left through remnants of Caledonian forest. It crosses the river three times, first at the Etnach turning, then back again half a mile on and just before crossing it for the third time it crosses the Mounth Road, running from Glen Esk to Ballater.

From this crossroads at 407897 it is possible to make a circuit back to Ballater. It also, of course, offers an alternative start to the walk. Where the B976 forks right at the monument by the Bridge of Muick outside Ballater, take the left-hand of the three roads which climbs uphill and degenerates into a cart track. Keep climbing. On a clear day there are fine views south-west to Lochnagar. The track circles Craig Vallich and turns east to cross the ridge, then descends to cross the headwaters of the Pollagach Burn to arrive at a gate in a fence on the right. The path descends south-east, then south to join up with the Glen Tanar approach just before the bridge over the Tanar.

The old bridge over the Water of Tanar. Inset, friendly advice ►
near Glen Tanar House.

Ca' canny
Doon the Brae

A Land Rover track now continues south to gain the west shoulder of Mount Keen (3079ft/939m) which can be climbed from here. The name means pleasant hill, as indeed it is. After one and a half miles the path descends steeply by the Ladder Burn to Glenmark Cottage. Just past this is a well where Queen Victoria slaked her thirst on a hot day in 1861. Now follow the Water of Mark down to the road at Invermark, just four miles (6.4km) west of Tarfside.

The Queen's Well where Victoria stopped for a drink in 1861. ▶

▼ *The southern end of the Mounth Road. The Queen's Well can be seen just above the third sheep from the right.*

Walk 44   Dinnet to Glen Esk by the Firmounth Road
OS 44: 467983 to 492798
13 miles (21km) with 2208ft (673m) of ascent

This walk has the same beginning as Walk 43 from Dinnet to the Bridge of Knockie. But here, instead of recrossing the River Tanar, go up through some super woods to join and then cross the Burn of Skinna. The path now climbs up the ridge between the Waters of Allachy and Skinna to Craigmahandle (1882ft/574m), then descends a little before rising once more to St Colme's Well, just to the west of Gannoch's summit (2399ft/731m). It is an easy climb from here to the top. Our path continues south. At the edge of a flat peaty area it goes close to the Tinker's Cairn, inscribed "W.E. 1814". Here a tinker murdered his wife. He was brought to trial and flatly denied ever crossing the Firmounth in his life, but when a witness for the prosecution stated that she had given the couple a drink of milk when they called at her house, he shouted out indignantly that it was only whey she had given them, not milk, and this sudden zeal for the whole truth sealed his fate.

The path continues south over Tampie (2371ft/723m) and meets up with the Fungle (see Walk 45) as it sweeps down to Tarfside.

Aboyne
Continuing east along the valley of the Dee from Dinnet brings us to Aboyne which takes its name from *boinne*, meaning rippling water. The castle to the north of the town once belonged to the Knights Templar and saw much activity during the Civil Wars and in Covenanting times. The present building dates from 1671. Close by

---

◄ *Invermark Castle, upper Glen Esk, a Lindsay bolt-hole with rounded corners, the lower part sixteenth-century, the upper two storeys added in the early seventeenth-century.*

▲ *The Bridge o'Ess, between Dinnet and Aboyne.*

the West Lodge are a couple of sculptured stones, one of which bears inscriptions in the ancient Celtic script of Ogham.

Walk 45   Aboyne to Glen Esk by the Fungle
OS 44: 525978 to 492798
12 miles (20km) with 2208ft (690m) of ascent

The Fungle is another named drove road which links Aboyne to the Firmounth. This means one has the choice of continuing on to Tarfside or returning in a great dog-leg to the Dee valley. Start from Birsemore on the B976 just across the river from Aboyne and at the junction turn right, then first left uphill past Parkside on a track following the Allt Dinnie, then crossing it at 518949.

(Incidentally, though the whole walk is conveniently contained on the OS Landranger 44 map, last revised in 1974, you will find the route up from Birsemore is much more clearly marked on the OS Landranger 37, also last revised in 1974.)

Now a rough path leads up to join the Fungle which runs uninterrupted south to sixteenth-century Birse Castle. Just before the castle you can go down the edge of a wood to the south until you find a good path across the tributaries of the Water of Feugh at 522903. Continue on the west bank of the burn as the track begins to veer south-west, eventually passing between Tampie and Mudlee Bracks. Just beyond this point it is joined on the right by the Firmounth Road described in Walk 44 which gives you the choice to continue to the Esk or return north to the Dee.

Lumphanan
A short distance to the north-west of Aboyne is the cheerful village of Lumphanan. Here, as every good Scot should know, Malcolm slew MacBeth in 1057. It is also notorious for the witch trials during James VI's reign. Just to the south-west at the farm of Cairnbeathie is

MacBeth's Stone and Well and MacBeth's Cairn is north of the village. After his last showdown with Malcolm Canmore the dying MacBeth was reputed to have drunk from the well, lain down to die by the stone, and been buried at the cairn. The stone, in the field by the old railway bridge, across the road from the Peel of Lumphanan, was probably an ancient standing stone. MacBeth was later exhumed and taken for more fitting burial at the royal burial ground on Iona, for he was a good and popular King of Scots, and the laws of MacBeth ensured justice in otherwise troubled times. Shakespeare was not

◄ *Looking toward the Peel of Lumphanan, beyond the car, from the stone marking the spot where MacBeth was struck down.*

▼ *The cairn to the north of Lumphanan where MacBeth was buried before being taken to Iona. Probably a much older burial cairn.*

strong on Scottish history and he got Lady MacBeth wrong too. But then he was writing political propaganda for James VI, a man of unpleasant habits and little time for ladies.

The Peel of Lumphanan is all that remains of a castle in which Edward I stayed in 1296. All that can be seen now is a huge artificial motte, which owed some of its protection to the marshy ground. The castle would have been a timber structure, the walls covered in mud to prevent them being fired and the whole affair encircled by a moat. It featured prominently in James VI's notorious witch trials.

If you enjoy collecting castles there are two more you can take in not very far north-west of Lumphanan – the sixteenth-century Z-plan fortalice of Corse Castle and the graceful five-turreted early seventeenth-century Craigievar just up the A980. But now let us leave this historical diversion and return to the River Dee and our next town to the east which is Banchory, starting point for our next four walks.

Banchory

The church of St Ternan proclaims Banchory's long history, starting as a Celtic missionary colony in the fifth century, and houses an ancient bell, associated with St Ternan, which was unearthed during improvement work on the Aberdeen water supply in 1920. An unusual feature of the present kirkyard is a circular morthouse, built in two storeys to foil bodysnatchers. There are also some interesting table stones. Today Dee lavender is a thriving local industry.

Just off the A93 to the east of the town is Crathes Castle which, together with its fine gardens, comes under the National Trust for Scotland. One Alexander Burnard was granted these lands by Robert the Bruce in 1323 and the Burnett family, his descendants, still display the Horn of Leys, reputed to have been presented to their ancestor by the Bruce himself.

Just north of Banchory stands the Hill of Fare (1545ft/
471m). It was here that the Battle of Corrichie was fought
in 1562. Mary Queen of Scots watched the spectacle from
the comfort of a natural granite seat on the hillside nearby,
still called Queen's Chair, and her Well is at a convenient
distance. This was her only visit into Scotland's northern
regions to break the Gordon stranglehold. The Gordon
chief died of apoplexy in his armour. His son, a hopeful
suitor of the Queen, was executed in Aberdeen, while
Mary watched. There is a memorial to the battle on the
B977.

Walk 46   Banchory to the Hill of Fare
OS 38: 685994 to 689032
4.5 miles (6.5km)

There are various ways up the Hill of Fare but it's best
to start to the west of the T-junction at Raemoir. Go
north past the remains of Cluny Castle (a late example of
an L-plan fortified house, circa 1666) and take the hill
road which meanders through trees, west of Craigrath
and so on to the spacious summit.

Walk 47   Banchory to Auchenblae by the Builg
Mounth
OS 45: 663910 to 727790
15 miles (24km) with 640ft (195m) of ascent

The Builg Mounth is another of the old roads marked on
Garden's map of 1776. Start by taking the road up the
Water of Feugh as far as the Bridge of Bogandreip. The
snaking road on the east bank via the Mill of Cammie is
quieter. Just before you reach the bridge, climb up the
forest road which curves east, then turns north. After two
miles (3.2km) through forest you come out on to open
ground again and follow the Builg Burn to traverse the
southern slopes of Little Kerloch south-east to arrive at

▲ *The ancient Bridge of Dye on the Cairn o' Mount road to Banchory. Tolls were exacted on this bridge by an Act of Parliament of 1681. Andrew Cant, the famous seventeenth-century Presbyterian divine, came from Glen Dye.*

the Builg which is between Tipperweir and Kerloch. There is no track for this section. Go down to the West Burn of Builg and follow it to arrive at a road just below Tipperty Farm, two miles (3.2km) from Auchenblae.

Walk 48   Banchory to Drumlithie by the Cryne Corse Mounth
OS 45: 703950 to 785810
15 miles (24km) with 736ft (224m) of ascent

Here is another old road marked on both Roy's map of 1755 and Garden's of 1776. This, or the Fungle, was possibly the route taken by Edward I in 1296. Cross the Water of Feugh to its east bank and take the road south up the river for a short way, but go left at the first junction. This road runs east and then south-east, passing on the right another Z-plan sixteenth-century fortalice,

Tilquhillie Castle. Further on a road to the right leads to West Mulloch and Mulloch Hill, sites of two prehistoric stone circles. Our way, however, goes on to join the A957, at which one turns right and follows the main road's bends for a mile to where a minor road runs south just past Spyhill Farm and the A957 sweeps sharply to the left. Follow this track south through the trees to Red Beard's Well. A tall TV mast here is a prominent landmark. Then continue round the east side of the Hill of Mossmaud and south along an old disused track towards the valley of the Cowie Water. Now follow the forest roads across the valley floor and ascend the other side to tracks leading to the Brae of Glenbervie.

Walk 49   Banchory to Glenbervie by the Stock Mounth
OS 45: 703950 to 766807
16 miles (25km) with 832ft (253m) of ascent

The Stock Mounth is the last of the trio of ancient roads we shall walk from Banchory. Take the road up the east side of the Water of Feugh to the Mill of Cammie as for Walk 47 and when you meet up with the Strachan road go east, then after half a mile turn uphill to reach Pitreadie. Go over the hills now in a south-easterly direction on a rough track for about a mile east of Kerloch. Then descend past the Well of Monluth to cross the top of Cowie Water and the east face of Leachie Hill to arrive at the Brae of Glenbervie. Just beyond is Bogjurgan Farm where Robert Burns' ancestors lived. Keep south by a minor road to Glenbervie.

We have now travelled to the eastern boundary of this book and, indeed, are within hailing distance of Stonehaven and the North Sea. Time to face west again and return to the Dee valley and the royal heart of Deeside, to Ballater which gives access south-west to Loch Muick.

Loch Muick

Loch Muick, two miles long by almost half a mile wide, is the biggest loch in the Cairngorms at an altitude of 1312ft (400m). It is also an excellent walking centre and accessible by an attractive minor road up the River Muick from Ballater. There is an Information Centre at the car park near the Spittal of Glenmuick which used to be a hospice for travellers along the Capel Mounth road. This is one of the oldest recorded roads in Scotland, first appearing on a map in 1360. Capel Mounth means the Mountain of the Horses.

Walk 50   Lock Muick to Glen Clova by the Capel Mounth Road
OS 44: 308850 to 285760
10 miles (16km) with 1600ft (487m) of ascent

Start from the Spittal but after a quarter of a mile take the path that heads uphill, signposted to Capel Mounth, which you reach at a height of 2275ft (693m). From here the way goes down in a series of zigzags to cross the Capel Burn, then descends into Glen Clova.

You can also reach Glen Clova by taking the path along the south shore of Loch Muick for a mile, then climbing a rough road south-west. At the plateau on top there are two small huts. The path continuing north-west offers a worthwhile diversion to Broad Cairn (3273ft/998m). The way to Glen Clova descends south to the old ruin of Bachnagairn with the Bachnagairn Falls close by. The path then follows first the south, then the east side of the river to where it is joined by the Capel Mounth track down to Braedownie.

These alternative routes make an excellent circular tour back to the Loch Muick car park.

Loch Muick and the division of the paths, left to Glen Clova via ▶
Capel Mounth, and right for the circuit of Loch Muick, Dubh
Loch or Broad Cairn.

Walk 51   Loch Muick to Dubh Loch by Glas-allt Shiel
OS 44: 308850 to 244826
6 miles (9.5km) with 787ft (240m) of ascent

A round tour of Loch Muick, which is about seven and a half miles, doesn't require any effort of ascent. Add to it a diversion to Dubh Loch and this excursion should have top priority on your itinerary. Near the west end of the loch is Glas-allt Shiel, a modest hunting lodge built by Queen Victoria in 1869. She used to like to stay here for a few nights each year to get away from it all, usually in October when the hills are covered in their first winter mantle. The house takes its name from the nearby Glas Allt, the Grey Burn, and if you climb a little way up the path beside it you will come to the spectacular Glas Allt Falls. Past the falls there is a path north-east which connects up with the route described in Walk 55, but for the present let us return to the west end of Loch Muick. The track for Dubh Loch goes past Glas-allt Shiel and is just over two miles from the lodge.

The setting is magnificent, a paradise for mountaineers and a joy for the walker to behold. Here is the highest and most continuous wall of rock in the Cairngorms, the great sweeps of smooth granite providing rock climbing routes of a high standard. On the north side of the Dubh Loch is Eagle's Rock which offers the rock gymnast about 492ft (150m) of steep south-facing granite.

◄ *The division of the glens, Glen Clova: Glen Doll and the Tolmount track to Braemar runs to the left. The Capel Mounth is to the right, as well as the route by the ruin of Bachnagairn Lodge which also leads to Loch Muick.*

Dubh Loch and the cliffs of Creag an Dubh Loch, the greatest ► *sweep of crags in the Cairngorms.*

When free of snow Central Gully, Creag an Dubh Loch provides ► ► *an easy scrambling route to the summit of Broad Cairn from Dubh Loch.*

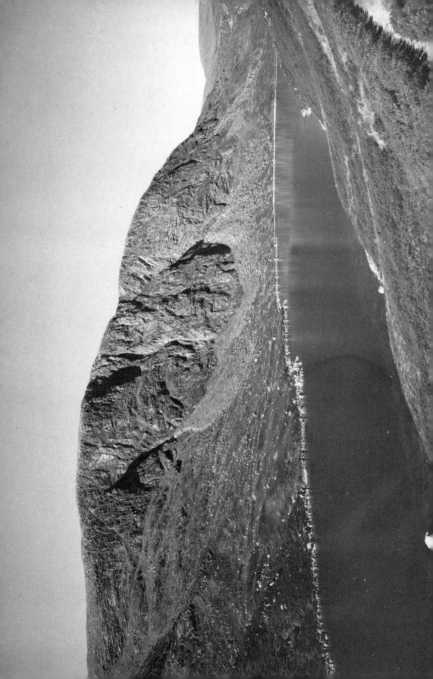

Lochnagar

Lochnagar has been immortalised by various prominent folk, the present Duke of Rothesay being but the most recent in an illustrious line. Lord Byron, who first climbed the mountain at the age of fifteen, later wrote:

> England! Thy beauties are tame and domestic
> To one who has roved o'er the mountains afar;
> Oh for the crags that are wild and majestic,
> The steep frowning glories of dark Lochnagar!

The area, which forms part of the Balmoral estate, was a favourite, too, with Queen Victoria who often wrote of it, and had the Prince Consort painted by John Phillip with Lochnagar as the background. The name properly refers to the lochan at the base of the north-east corrie, and means Lochan of the Noisy Sound. It is shown on Blaeu's *Atlas* of 1654 and in 1771 Thomas Pennant mentions Laghin y gair. It is not difficult to walk to the summit (3788ft/1155m) and the most popular route is from the Spittal of Glen Muick.

◄ *Lochnagar, one of the jewels of the White Mounth.*

▼ *The summit plateau and the steep cliffs of Lochnagar.*

Walk 52   Loch Muick to Lochnagar
OS 44: 308850 to 245861
11 miles (17km) with 2500ft (762m) of ascent

Follow the signs to Lochnagar which take you north-west from the Loch Muick car park across the river past Allt-na-Giubhsaich Lodge. Head west and up to the col between Meikle Pap (3213ft/980m) and a zigzag path called the Ladder. It is well worth going first to the top of Meikle Pap for a super view into the North-East Corrie. Then carry on up the Ladder to the first plateau. Now follow the edge of the corrie leading to Cac Carn Mor and beyond, the summit, Cac Carn Beag. (Yes, Beag really is five metres higher than Mor!) The path is easily followed for most of the way, but unless you are a mountaineer, don't attempt the ascent, or any other high peaks, should snow be lying.

You may return to Loch Muick by the same route. Alternatively, it is possible to go south-east from Cac Carn Mor to the headwaters of the Glas Allt and carry on down to the Glas Allt Falls. But make sure you locate the path on the true right of the stream before continuing the descent. This option is some two miles (3.2km) longer than the approach route. Again, if you don't mind reading directions backwards, you can try Walks 53, 54 and 55 in reverse. But the other way round they are three splendid approaches to the mountains.

Walk 53   Ballochbuie to Lochnagar
OS 43, 44: 185910 to 245861
5 miles (8km) with 2755ft (840m) of ascent

This is a super way to climb Lochnagar, being less crowded and the lower forest is magnificent. Starting at the west end of the Invercauld Bridge, a private road goes on past the Old Bridge of Dee to reach a crossroads. Keep straight on at this and the next crossroads to a road which

▲ *The old six-arch military bridge across the Dee at Invercauld near Braemar was built in 1752. The new Invercauld Bridge which carries the A93 is to the right where the river bends to the north.*

leads up south-east close to the Falls of Garbh Allt, which are just off this road. (There is an alternative route – sometimes locked – to this spot from the white suspension bridge across the Dee to the north.) Follow the road up the Feindallacher Burn close to where the Allt a' Choire Dubh meets it. Now go easily on the path up Smugglers Shank to crest the point between the two streams and thence on to Carn an t-Sagairt Beag. Follow easily east along the plateau to Stuic and onwards to the summit of Lochnagar.

◄ *Dark Lochnagar, as seen from the road to Loch Muick.*

Walk 54 Glen Callater to Lochnagar
OS 43, 44: 156883 to 245861
9 miles (15km) with 2492ft (762m) of ascent

It is three miles to Loch Callater from the bridge of Auchallater on the A93 – a case for hiring a bicycle in Braemar maybe. Just before the old lodge at the north-west end of the loch the Lochnagar path goes uphill, then angles across Creag an Loch. (On the 7th Series OS 43 Creag an Loch is wrongly placed. It should be at 193845.) Beyond the path toils round the south side of Carn an t-Sagairt Mor, the Big Hill of the Priest, to go down into the top basin of the Allt an Dubh Loch. From here it's easy going on to the plateau of Am Monadh Geal and you continue north-east to Stuic (3583ft/1093m) and on to the summit which is 330ft (100m) higher.

Balmoral and Crathie
Balmoral is, of course, famous for Balmoral Castle, the summer retreat of the royal family. The Balmoral estate, an old Gordon property, was at first leased by Queen Victoria, who bought it in 1848, dismantled the original structure and built the new castle. Close by, still on the south bank of the Dee, is Easter Balmoral with its diminutive store – 'By Royal Appointment'. At the back of this hamlet lurks the Royal Lochnagar Distillery of John Begg fame, and the starting point to Walk 56.

Across the Dee is the main Deeside highway, the A93, and Crathie with its church where generations of royalty have kept their peace with God. It is the most recent of five places of worship that have acted as parish church. Its predecessor, some 400 yards (125m) down towards the river, is worth a visit. There's not much to see of the church now, but there are some interesting old tomb-stones outside, one dated 1698, and also the grave of Queen Victoria's favourite Highland servant, fulsomely remembered:

▲ *Balmoral Castle, a favoured royal residence.*

JOHN BROWN'S GRAVE
This Stone Is Erected In Affectionate
And Grateful Remembrance Of
JOHN BROWN
The Devoted and Faithful
Personal Attendant And Beloved Friend of
QUEEN VICTORIA
IN WHOSE SERVICE HE HAS BEEN FOR 34 YEARS
BORN AT CRATHIENAIRD,
8TH DEC. 1826;
DIED AT WINDSOR CASTLE, 27th MARCH, 1883.
"That friend on whose fidelity you count, that friend given you
by circumstances over which you have no control, was God's
own gift."

"Well done, good and faithful servant,
Thou has been faithful over a few things
I will make thee ruler over many things
Enter thou into the joy of the Lord."

▼ *Balmoral Castle was purchased by Queen Victoria in 1848. She
had the old fortalice dismantled and the new Scottish baronial
building erected at a cost of £100,000.*

▲ *Crathie Church, place of royal worship at Balmoral.*

Walk 55   Balmoral to Lochnagar
OS 44: 264942 to 245861
6 miles (10km) with 2902ft (885m) of ascent

This walk offers some of the best views of Lochnagar. Starting from the village of Balmoral on the south side of the Dee, take the private road from the shop which goes through the gap of Dubh Chlais, the Dark Furrow, and follow it across the moor where you come to the turnoff for Gelder Shiel. Now you can either go directly on to where the path from Allt-na-Giubhsaich comes in from the east and continue round the head of Coire na Ciche to reach the summit of Lochnagar, as in Walk 52, or you can take the path to Gelder Shiel and continue past it alongside the Lochnagar Burn to arrive at the loch. This is the more spectacular way to view the cliffs. It is possible to traverse round the loch and contour Meikle Pap to meet up with the Allt-na-Giubhsaich path.

Walk 56   Balmoral to Loch Muick
OS 44: 267938 to 308850
8 miles (12km) with 675ft (206m) of ascent

From Easter Balmoral take the road by the Royal Lochnagar Distillery for half a mile, then climb the hill to the south-east and traverse the ease side of Tom Bad a' Mhonaidh. Now head south to the gap south of Meall Gorm and so on down to Glen Muick. From here walk alongside the river to the Allt-na-Giubhsaich, keep straight on for Loch Muick, or turn left across the river for the Spittal of Glenmuick car park.

Braemar
Like Balmoral, Braemar owes much of its fame to royalty and in particular to the renowned Braemar Royal Highland Gathering each September. This spectacle has roots going right back to the days of Malcolm Canmore in the eleventh century who used to hold competitions to select the fleetest athletes for his personal messenger service and the best swordsmen for his army. The race was run up Creag Choinnich, the hill across the road from Braemar Castle. A story survives from King Malcolm's day of the three MacGregor brothers. They were hot favourites and two of them entered the race. The eldest had already shown his good MacGregor reiving mettle by pursuing a wild boar from Glen Callater through Glen Cluny up into the Cairngorms and back to Balmoral all in one day. The

Braemar Castle is situated just outside the village on the Balmoral road. It was built in 1628 upon a much earlier structure and is open to the public.

youngest son arrived late, after the race had started, and had to plead with the King to let him participate. Yet despite his self-imposed handicap, the youngest Mac-Gregor caught up with and passed all the rest of the field, beat his brothers, collected the prize and no doubt also got the job as royal postie.

From such misty beginnings 20,000 spectators now gather in this village each year to witness the caber tossing, shot putting, piping, dancing and other Highland skills which make up the gathering. If you want to try your hill-running skills on Creag Choinnich, turn off the A93 at St Margaret's Church, and continue to the gate and stile at the foot of the hill. Take the left-hand path up the hill. The wider one, going straight ahead, leads to the Queen's Drive.

The village should really be called Castleton of Braemar after the stronghold of Kindrochit Castle which, even in ruins, imparts an aura of power. It stands above the Linn

---

The remains of Kindrochit Castle, Braemar, dating from the early fourteenth century, though there was a castle on this site in Malcolm Canmore's time. ▶

▼ *The gallows tree by the Dee near Braemar.*

of the Clunie and had its own mill. Some of the surviving structure dates from the fourteenth century, but there was a castle here even before the time of Malcolm Canmore, as there is evidence to suggest that Angus MacFergus, King of the Picts, visited the stronghold, as did Kenneth MacAlpin, the first King of Scots and Picts. You can't go much further back than that in Scottish history! The bridge across the Clunie close to the castle links what are in effect two villages, Castleton and Auchendryne. On the Castleton side of the bridge stands the Invercauld Arms. This is built on the site of the Raising of the Standard in 1715 by Bobbing John, Earl of Mar, in support of the Old Pretender. A more modern edifice close by was erected by the Deeside Field Club to commemorate the coronation of 'Elizabeth Queen of Scots'. Opposite the Invercauld Galleries is a house where in 1881 Robert Louis Stevenson wrote part of *Treasure Island*.

Braemar Castle, a short way out of the village on the A93 to Balmoral, looks as if it has been transplanted from Disneyland. The original structure dates from 1628, built by the eighteenth Earl of Mar. The Black Colonel, John Farquharson of Inverey, burned it in 1689. The upper third was rebuilt after the 1745 Rising when it had been burned by the government. Below the floor of the vaulted basement is a dungeon which doesn't merit any accommodation award. The castle is open to the public, and among the treasures on display is the world's biggest cairngorm stone weighing fifty-two pounds (23kg).

The kilt is still to be seen in Braemar, especially during the Highland Gathering. But this was not always the case. After the '45 Rising the Disarming Act of 1747 made it a punishable offence to wear one. All highlanders had to take this oath: "I . . . do swear I have not, nor shall have in my possession, any gun, sword, pistol or arm whatsoever, and never use tartan, plaid, or any part of the Highland garb; and if I do, may I be cursed in my

An historic plaque in the Invercauld Arms, Braemar. ▶

209

ON THIS SPOT
THE EARL OF MAR
RAISED HIS STANDARD OF REBELLION
1715

undertakings, may I never see my wife or children or relatives: may I be killed in battle as a coward, and lie without Christian burial in a strange land far from the graves of my kindred."

Walk 57   Braemar to Morrone
OS 43: 144905 to 133887
5 miles (8km) with 1180ft (360m) of ascent

You can start from the Princess Royal Park where the Highland Gathering takes place and follow paths up through the trees to a knoll boasting a host of views on a fine day. Close by there is a path from the croft of Tomintoul which leads to the summit (2817ft/859m). Morrone probably means Big Nose. According to legend there was until recent times on the summit the ruins of a shieling belonging to Cailleach Bheur, the Winter Hag, who used to milk the hinds for her sustenance. Today, more practically, the summit houses a radio repeater belonging to the local mountain rescue team.

You can also ascend – or indeed descend – by Glen Clunie on a rough track from the minor road across the Clunie Water from Auchallater. Alternatively, you can go back to Braemar by Chapel Brae on a path to the north through birch and juniper.

Walk 58   Braemar to Tomintoul
OS 43, 36: 186911 to 171184
20 miles (32km)

Take the A93 east to Invercauld Bridge and go up the signposted road to Keiloch, then turn left along the road which runs north-west behind Invercauld House. Here an old drove road leads north, running east of Creag a'

◄ *Invercauld House.*

Chait. At 180981 take the left-hand fork and continue north over the Bealach Dearg which lies between Carn Liath and Culardoch, then drop down to the River Gairn. Cross the footbridge and follow the track north-east along the river to the east side of Loch Builg, then north to Inchrory. From here it is seven miles (11km) north to Tomintoul, following the east bank of the River Avon (the first half of Walk 37 in reverse).

Alternatively you can take a slightly shorter route starting from Inver (234938), between Crathie and Invercauld on the A93. Go west and north to Ratlich. From here head north, traversing Carn Moine an Tighearn, then across the eastern side of Culardoch. Continue north to slant down by Tom a' Chuir to reach the River Gairn and the Invercauld–Tomintoul route just south of Loch Builg.

Walk 59   Braemar to Ben Avon
OS 43, 36: 186911 to 133018
10 miles (16km) with 2788ft (850m) of ascent

Start as for Walk 58 from Invercauld Bridge and bypass Invercauld House. From here a path continues north-west up the scenic An Slugain which means The Gullet, past the ruins of Slugain Lodge. Beyond the slope runs west into Quoich Water, but keep to the lazily-angled path heading north to the Stone of the Priest, Clach a' Chleirich, which is nothing more than a large boulder on the slope. Next take the glen to the north-north-east which rises to the bealach, or saddle, between Ben Avon and Cnap a' Chleirich at 125013. This feature is called the Notch or Sneck. Below you to the north is probably the finest corrie in the country, Garbh Choire, the Rough Corrie, an exquisite profusion of rock architecture which, because of its remoteness, is not often visited.

Running from it, further down is An Slochd Mor, the Great Pit, a wild glen which storms up from Glen Avon.

It is possible to walk down the scree slopes (if they are free from snow) into the Slochd Mor and thence down to the Avon, heading east to Inchrory and on to Tomintoul (the start of Walk 36 in reverse), but it is a long way.

However, to continue with the ascent of Ben Avon, go east from the Sneck for 533 yards up the gravelly, stony, turfy incline to reach the plateau, then north-east to the highest craggy point at 3840ft (1171m). The peak is named Leabaidh an Daimh Bhuidhe on the maps, which means the Couch of the Yellow Stag.

You can return by the ascent route, or descend to the south-south-west past Stob Dubh an Eas Bhig, which is a black tor, then across the plateau which is to the north-west of the higher angled slope at Carn Eas. (The slope to the south, along the rim of the plateau, carries snow until late in the year and can be dangerous.) From this plateau, head down to the Slugain, avoiding the rim of the plateau. A more pleasant route back is to descend to the south-east into the verdant upper corrie of the Allt an Eas Mhoir. One should watch out for snow here, too, as the slope to the west of the stream occasionally displays a steep snow wall. Carry on down by the leaping burn to gain the path along the River Gairn to return to Invercauld by the Bealach Dearg, as in Walk 59 in reverse.

Walk 60   Braemar to Culardoch
OS 43, 36: 186911 to 194989
10 miles (16km) with 1928ft (588m) of ascent

This heathery domed mountain (2952ft/900m) to the north-north-east of Braemar is accessible from the Braemar to Tomintoul Walk 58, or from its alternative start at Inver. Go one way, come back the other. If you go up to the Bealach Dearg on the Invercauld–Inchrory path, strike off to the north-east to reach the summit. An alternative is to take the earlier track to the right beyond

Creag a' Chait which approaches Culardoch from the south up the wide nose.

Nearer to Invercauld House Craig Leek (2082ft/635m) offers more fine views. The name means Flagstone Rock, possibly from the diorite cliff on its easterly aspect. To get to the top walk up through the pines from Keiloch.

Travelling west from Braemar along the minor road south of the Dee brings you to the Victoria Bridge and across it on the right is Mar Lodge, now a hotel for sportsmen who keep up the tradition observed in 1618 by John Taylor, the Thames waterman poet, who walked all the way to Braemar and described the lavish deer drives organised on the estate of the Earl of Mar:

> those foresaid scouts, which are called the Tinchell, do bring down the deer. But as the proverb says of a bad cooke so these Tinchell men doe lick their own fingers; for besides their bows and arrowes, which they carry with them, wee can heare now and then a harquerbusse or musket goe off, which they doe seldom discharge in vaine. Then after we had stayed three houres, or thereabouts, we might perceive the deer appeare on the hills round about us (their heads making a shew like a wood), which, being followed close by the Tinchell, are charged down into the valley where wee lay. Then all the valley on each side being waylaid with a hundred couple of strong Irish greyhounds, they are let loose as occasion serves upon the hearde of deere, that with dogs, gunnes, arrowes, durks, and daggers, in the space of two houres, four score fat deere were slaine, which after are disposed of some one way and some another, twenty or thirty miles; and more than enough left for us to make merrey with all at our rendevouse.

Near Victoria Bridge is the Farquharsons' private gallows tree, now on its last legs and supported by guy wires. Many erring chiels, or young men, ended their days suspended from it. In the fifteenth century Lamont of Inverey hung from a branch, despite his mother's entreaties for mercy. As her plea was ignored she cursed the Farquharsons in Gaelic which loses little in translation:

> This tree wil flourish high and broad,
> Green as it grows today,
> When from the banks o' Bonnie Dee
> Clan Fhionnlagh's all away.

▼ *The Colonel's Bed and adjoining water supply. Take care on the descent to this bedroom. Inset, a terse direction.*

Like other such curses in the Highlands this one too seems to have worked. By 1876 the family had become extinct in the male line, when the tree was still vigorous, but unemployed.

The Black Colonel was one of the most notorious Farquharsons. He once escaped naked from his house when the government troops burnt it down and made a prodigious leap across the Ey which was in spate at the time. This spot, about a mile upstream from the present bridge, is known as Drochaid an Leum, the Bridge of the Leap. Glen Ey also contains the Colonel's Bed, about three miles south of Inverey. The way is signposted, but take care descending into the gorge as it is now rather dangerous. The bed was where the Black Colonel holed up after the Battle of Killiecrankie. It would have made a draughty boudoir as it is a water-worn ledge just above the level of the river, but from it you can sometimes see salmon in the deep pool below.

Walk 61   Inverey to Carn Liath
OS 43: 087892 to 036868
8 miles (13km) with 1640ft (502m) of ascent

The ascent of Carn Liath (2683ft/818m) offers a fine circular walk, but should not be attempted in the stalking season. From the old bridge across the River Ey at 087884, follow the road up the true left of the river, cross a stile and ascend through a plantation on a Land Rover road. Continue on the path to the plateau, then head north to the summit cairn. You can continue along the ridge to the north-east to Carn na Moine and descend to the Carn Liath track from there, or strike out north-west from the summit of Carn Liath and go down the slopes by Duncan Gray's Burn, to a footbridge across the Dee at White-bridge which allows a circuit back to Inverey by the Linn of Dee. Duncan Gray who had the burn named after him is the hapless hero of a song about unrequited love:

Duncan Gray cam' here to woo,
    Ha, ha, the wooing o't,
On blythe Yule-night when we were fou,
    Ha, ha, the wooing o't:
Maggie coost her head fu' heigh,
Look'd asklent and unco skeigh,
Gart poor Duncan stand abeigh;
    Ha, ha, the wooing o't.

Duncan fleech'd and Duncan pray'd;
    Ha, ha, the wooing o't,
Meg was deaf as Ailsa Craig,
    Ha, ha, the wooing o't;
Duncan sigh'd baith out and in,
Grat his e'en baith blear't an' blin',
Spak o' lowpin o'er a linn;
    Ha, ha, the wooing o't.

But fortunately he thought better of this and some verses later:

Time and Chance are but a tide,
    Ha, ha, the wooing o't,
Slighted love is sair to bide,
    Ha, ha, the wooing o't:
"Shall I, like a fool," quoth he,
"For a haughty hizzie die?
She may gae to – France for me!"
    Ha, ha, the wooing o't.

Walk 62   Inverey to Glenmore Lodge or Nethy Bridge by the Lairig an Laoigh
OS 43, 36: 068898 to 988096 or 013197
30 miles (48km) with 1568ft (490m) of ascent

The Lairig an Laoigh is another of the famous drove roads and means the Pass of the Calves. Our earlier walks have already crossed it on more than one occasion. Its suitability for driving calves supports the fact that it is one of the routes with relatively easy going. But relatively is as relatively does in the Cairngorms and no long walk in this area should be taken lightly.

The Lairig an Laoigh can still be treacherous in bad weather, as a party of Morayshire Militia found in December 1804. They were on leave from Edinburgh Castle and on their way home to Forres for Hogmanay. The good folk of Braemar urged them not to set out. A dance was even arranged to delay their departure. But the seven men were determined to be home for the New Year festivities. Despite drifting snow they made it to beyond Lochan a' Bhainne. There they made the mistake of following the Glasath instead of heading over the east shoulder of Bynack More. It was two years before the last body was found in the great Drumochter. So you have been warned!

Start from the locked gate in Glen Lui and follow the path up the glen to Derry Lodge. About a mile east of here is the Allt a' Mhadaidh Allaidh, the Wolf's Burn. It was here that the last wolf seen in the Forest of Mar was killed about 1650.

Cross the Derry by the footbridge just beyond the lodge. For the next four miles the route is the same as the approach to Ben Macdui from Derry Lodge, described in Walk 28. The path leads north for a mile through superb pines before turning left away from the stream. Near here, though not visible from the path, are fine waterfalls. Beyond you come to a bridge, cross this to the east side of the Derry. Just above is the site of the old Derry Dam, used at one time for log flotation.

The falls in lower Glen Lui, with a salmon ladder to the left of ▶
the falls.

Stags in velvet near Derry Lodge. The Lairig Ghru runs up the ▶
valley to the right.

This dam was constructed by a strong man of Upper Deeside called Alexander Davidson. Once he got lost in these hills in a blizzard and came across a small burn which he knew must lead him down to safety. However, he was exhausted and exposed and could not determine which way the stream flowed. Upon chucking snowballs into the water he was amazed to observe that they appeared to float uphill but, knowing that this must be an hallucination, he followed the direction the snowballs took and eventually reached the safety of lower ground. It is interesting to note that now such a trick of vision is recognised, though not always by the victim, as a symptom of exposure. From the bridge a Land Rover track leads back down the east side of the river to Derry Lodge, which offers an alternative shorter walk.

Past the bridge follow the continuation of this road northwards for 1.2 miles and take the continuing path to the footbridge which spans the Glas Allt Mor, the Big Green Burn. Beyond the path forks, the left branch heading up into Coire Etchachan and superb cliff scenery of Walks 28 and 29. The right fork takes you to the Lairig an Laoigh at 2427ft (740m), the pass between Beinn a' Chaorainn and Beinn Mheadhoin, then on to Dubh Lochan and the River Avon. Beware, this ford over the Avon can be dangerous when the water is in spate. It is called the ford of the Fianna or the Fingalians. There is an emergency shelter on the north bank.

The next stretch of route has already been described in reverse as one of Walk 30's approaches to Loch Avon. Keep going north, past Lochan a' Bhainne, then across the start of the Water of Caiplich. From here you should be careful to avoid the fate of the Morayshire Militia and take the path which slants uphill to the left to cross the

◀ ◀ *Red deer near Derry Lodge, the start of the Lairig Ghru and Lairig an Laoigh walks.*

◀ *The footbridge across the Derry Burn at Derry Lodge.*

east shoulder of Bynack More at an altitude of 2525ft (770m). Now go north-west across the plateau for two miles to descend to the River Nethy at Bynack Stable.

The quickest and in my opinion the finest way back to civilisation from here is past Loch a' Gharbh-choire down through the pines on the wide track skirting lovely Lochan Uaine to Glenmore Lodge. A further route is to cut over to Ryvoan about half a mile beyond Loch a' Gharbh-choire, on past Rynettin, a superb place overlooking the Abernethy pine forest, and on to Forest Lodge. A short distance (1km) to the west of the lodge you arrive at the public road to Nethy Bridge.

Walk 63   Braemar to Carn na Drochaide
OS 43: 115914 to 128939
4 miles (7km) with 1640ft (502m) of ascent

The public road from the Linn of Dee along the north of the river ends at Allanaquoich. This is the point from which to climb Carn na Drochaide (2683ft/818m), the Hill of the Bridge, though the nearest one from Braemar is the Victoria Bridge, not exactly close by. If the river is very low, however, it is possible to ford it where it runs near the road at 144914. The way to the top of Carn na Drochaide is self-evident and the views rewarding.

Walk 64   Braemar to Beinn a' Bhuird
OS 43, 36: 115914 to 094006
7.5 miles (12km) with 2624ft (800m) of ascent

The ascent of Beinn a' Bhuird (3924ft/1196m) is easy to follow as a rough road toils up almost to the top of the mountain. Start from Allanaquoich again and take the path that follows the Quoich to a bridge, passing en route the now damaged Punch Bowl pothole. It is said that the Earl of Mar filled it with punch for his supporters in the Rising of 1715. *Quoich* means cup.

Where you cross the Allt an Dubh Ghleann the glen divides. The right branch goes up the Quoich Water, which it crosses, then doubles back to return to Allanaquoich on the east side of the stream. The road you want to get to the summit of Beinn a' Bhuird is straight on through the pines of Alltan na Beinne. Now climb the zigzags and dip down to An Diollaid. (There is an old path running up here which takes a rising line beneath most of the zigzags.) The road still toils upwards to run out of steam at 3542ft (1080m) and from its expiry point it is an easy walk to either or both the tops of Beinn a' Bhuird. As with all the higher Cairngorms, don't venture on to the tops if snow is lying, or if the weather is unsettled.

The A93 leads south from Braemar on the line of the old military road, up Glen Clunie, over the Cairnwell, and now bypassing the Devil's Elbow which has been 'doctored'. It then eases down on the well graded highway to the Spittal of Glenshee. Two miles out of Braemar on this road, opposite the route down from (or up) Morrone at Auchallater is the track to Glen Clova via the Tolmount.

Walk 65   Glen Callater to Glen Clova by Tolmount
OS 43, 44: 156883 to 327730
18 miles (29km) with 1741ft (531m) of ascent

Head south-east up to Loch Callater. (The hill path to Lochnagar (Walk 54) starts from the north end of the loch by the lodge.) It was into this lovely valley that Queen Victoria made her last expedition with Prince Albert in October 1861. A bulldozed road runs along the south side of the loch wherein are many pike. Continue up the Allt an Loch which goes steeply up to the pass at 3000ft (914m).

It is also possible to climb several of the peaks to the west, Carn an Tuirc 3340ft (1019m), Cairn of Claise 3484ft (1064m) and Tolmount 3143ft (958m). A rough

▲ *Jock's Road, a stretch of the Tolmount path in Glen Doll.*

road toils up Carn Tuirc Beag on the north-west of Loch Kander and offers a good springboard for these summits. Or you can climb Tolmount from the pass itself.

Beyond the pass the path, turning almost at right angles, ascends to 3014ft (918m) before dipping down as Jock's Road into Glen Doll where it meets up with a forest road down Glen Doll to Glen Clova.

Walk 66   Cairnwell Burn Bridge to Glen Isla by the Monega Pass
OS 43: 147808 to 191697
11 miles (17km) with 2700ft (822m) of ascent

Continuing down the A93 from Braemar, this walk east through to Glen Isla begins where the main road crosses the Cairnwell Burn seven and a half miles south of Braemar. Follow the east bank of the stream for half a mile and where the winter sports track leads off north-east to the ski tow on Carn an Tuirc, we keep going south-east round Glas Maol (3503ft/1068m), along a bulldozed road which takes us along the crags overlooking Caenlochan Glen to swing south of Monega Hill. Then it's downhill to arrive close to Tulchan in Glen Isla, and two miles on to the road-end at Auchavan.

Two miles further south down the A93 and you have a pair of mountains to climb, one on either side of the road. Park in the Cairnwell car park, which in the winter provides popular skiing facilities and a number of access roads. Without its white mantle this area isn't so inviting, but it offers these 'instant' hill walks.

▼ *Forter Castle, 'the Bonnie Hoose o'Airlie', destroyed by Argyll during the Covenant wars.*

Walk 67 The Cairnwell and Carn Aosda
OS 43: 135775 and 135793
3 miles (5km) with 750ft (228m) of ascent

If you start from the Cairnwell car park you are at 2148ft (655m) already. You can succumb to the chairlift and arrive just beneath the Cairnwell summit if you like, but to hike from the road is a mere 767ft (234m), so why not do this and feel righteous at 3060ft (933m). To reach Aosda you take the ridge northwards, losing 500ft (152m) and climbing some 450ft (137m) to gain the Aosda's top at 3007ft (917m). There are bulldozed roads and similar penalties of progress scattered about this route visible to the summer visitors.

The Battle of Cairnwell took place in 1644. Some Argyll ruffians, ironically known as Cleansers, had spent the summer lifting most of the cattle from Glen Isla and Glen Shee. The locals enlisted the help of MacKenzie of Dalmore and their combined force scrubbed out the Cleansers. An archer called Cam Ruadh particularly excelled at picking off the Cleansers one by one. But poetic justice awarded him an arrow on his own backside. As he returned to his home in Braemar the local good ladies called to him to observe that he had an arrow in his posterior. He is reputed to have replied tersely, "I myself know that." His wife successfully extracted it by placing one foot either side of the offending shaft and heaving before Cam Ruadh could sit down to a large celebratory venison dinner.

Walk 68 Glas Maol and Creag Leacach
OS 43: 167766 and 155746
5.5 miles (8.5km) with 1376ft (419m) of ascent

From the Cairnwell car park there is a well marked route east over Meall Odhar Beag, or to the south of this peaklet to the winter ski area, then directly up to the plateau and follow the remains of a fence which goes most of the way to the summit at 3504ft (1068m). From here you can meander to the south-south-west down the stony ridge to gain the top of Creag Leacach (3237ft/987m). But don't try descending from here. A better route back to base takes you from Glas Maol south-west on to Meall Gorm and reaches the road at Rhiedorrach, the Dark Shieling.

Glen Shee

Glen Shee means Glen of the Fairy and the Spittal of Glenshee was once a hospice. There has been a hostelry of some description at the Spittal for centuries. The old road here, and indeed large sections of the modern highway, follow the line of the old military road constructed between 1750 and 1754 from Blairgowrie to Grantown. There is an interesting old church in Glen Shee and an early account from *Chambers' Journal* describes a church service there 140 years ago.

There were no seats, but here and there a big stone placed, and as things of great luxury, there were two or three sticks laid from one of these to another. The floor was literally paved with human bones, and I saw that the dogs had gnawed the ends of many of them by way of amusing themselves in the time of worship. There were also hundreds of human teeth, while in the northwest corner of the Chapel there was an open grave, which had stood so for nearly three months. It had been made in the preceding December for a young man, who had died in the braes of Angus, but it came on such a terrible storm that they could not bring the corpse, so they buried him where he was, and left this grave standing ready for the next. When the service was over, the minister gathered the collection for the poor on the green, in the crown of his hat, and neither men nor women thought of dispersing, but stood in clubs about the Chapel, conversing some of them for upwards of an hour. I have seen many people who appeared to pay more attention to the service, but I never saw any who appeared to enjoy the crack after the sermon so much.

'Bonnie Glen Shee.' The Spittal of Glenshee with the old military ▶ bridge.

Walk 69   Spittal of Glenshee to Kirkmichael
OS 43: 110699 to 080600
8.5 miles (14km)

Walk south-west from the hotel up the Coire Lairige to pass along the north side of An Lairig (2232ft/680m). Now go down the Allt Doire nan Eun and on to Dirnanean and Enochdu where you can cross the River Ardle to Dalreoch and take the track of Walks 3 and 4 to Kirkmichael, avoiding the A924.

Glen Isla
Our descent of the A93 down the Shee Water stops when the B951 leads off to the east through Cray to Glen Isla, a quiet glen, lesser known than the winter sports-fixated Glen Shee to the west and Glens Prosen, Clova and Esk to the east. It is a verdant, tranquil valley and, if you continue east when the B951 bends south, you will come to the ruins of Forter Castle, 'the Bonnie Hoose o' Airlie' of the ballad. Here in the seventeenth century during the Covenanting wars the Countess of Airlie was forced to watch as the Earl of Argyll plundered and burnt the castle, but not before, if the ballad is to be believed, she had harangued him roundly from the battlements:

> "Eleven bairns I hae born
> And the twelfth ne'er saw his daddie,
> But though I had gotten as mony again,
> They sud a' gang to fecht for Charlie.

> "Gin my guid lord had been at hame,
> As he's awa' for Charlie,
> There dursna a Campbell o' a' Argyll
> Set a fit on the bonnie hoose o' Airlie."

> He's ta'en her by the milk-white hand,
> But he didna lead her fairly;
> He led her up to the tap o' the hill,
> Whaur she saw the burnin' o' Airlie.

▲ *Glen Isla and the ruined Ogilvie castle at Forter.*

The smoke and flame they rose so high,
The walls they were blackened fairly;
And the lady laid her doon on the green to dee,
When she saw the burnin' o' Airlie.

Walk 70 Glen Isla to Glen Prosen and Glen Clova
OS 43, 44: 187648 to 357697
16 miles (25km) with 670ft (204m) of ascent

From the road up Glen Isla just north of Folda cut off north-east about 100 yards (93m) short of the bridge. Carry on up the track, over a ridge to the north-east of Auchintaple Loch. The path now descends and can't make up its mind how to cross the Muckle Burn Moor. Its final choice is not clear. However, head for the low point between Craigie Law and Bada Croinard. Here you will find a stile (223657) and on the far side a track going into the forest. This leads on over the low point, the 'glach' and you gain a rough road which takes you south to Glenmarkie Lodge.

It is also possible to reach this point from Kirkton of Glen Isla, starting from East Mill Farm (224604) and taking the forest road.

Continuing to Glen Clova from Glenmarkie Lodge, carry on eastwards, then up through the Moss of Glanny where there is the choice of a track or a forest road. Whichever you choose will bring you to Glenhead Lodge. Now head to the north-east through Drumshade forestry plantation and thence over the Hill of Strone to reach the Glen Prosen's main highway at Cormuir.

Glen Prosen is a lovely Angus glen. Close to the entrance on Tulloch Hill is the Airlie Memorial Tower (375614) commemorating the eleventh Earl of Airlie who died in 1900 on Diamond Hill in the Second Boer War. He fell leading a cavalry charge and his dying words were, "Moderate your language, please, Sergeant."

To carry on to Glen Clova, go down the road from Cormuir for about one and a half miles and cross the river to Inchmill where you follow the east bank of the Burn of Inchmill to Drumwhern and descend to Glen Clova and the B955 close to Eggie.

Walk 71   Glen Isla to Glen Doll
OS 44: 224604 to 287757
13 miles (21km) with 1100ft (335m) of ascent

Start at East Mill Farm and take the forest road to Glenmarkie Lodge. Then walk north through the forestry up Glen Finlet on a rough road and, when this runs out at the top of the glen, head north-east up over the low point to descend into Glen Prosen at the ruins of Kilbo. You can also reach this point by walking up Glen Prosen, which gives you the option of a circular tour.

However, to continue to Glen Doll, go north-east taking an indistinct track, confidently marked Kilbo Path on OS 44, which may require some concentration to follow. This should take you to a pass south of the Shank of

Drumfollow. The path runs beside the Burn of Kilbo and on into Glendoll Forest and Glen Doll. Here, where Glen Doll joins Glen Clova at Braedownie is also the end of Walk 50 which linked Deeside and Loch Muick to Glen Clova by the historic Capel Mounth Road. From Braedownie, follow the minor road down to Clova to reach the B955.

Walk 72   Kilbo Path, Tolmount, Loch Esk to Glen Clova
OS 44: 253738 to 287757
10 miles (16km) with 1990ft (606m) of ascent

A worthwhile diversion from the Kilbo Path is to climb Mayar (3043ft/928m), the summit to the north-west which commands a fine view. From here you can continue to the shepherds' track at Dun Hillocks and slant down to join Jock's Road back down Glen Doll, or keep north a little longer to Little Kilrannoch, Tom Buidhe and Tolmount. From Tolmount bear east across Jock's Road to Loch Esk, then on to the ruined Bachnagairn Lodge, to descend to Moulzie and Braedownie.

Glen Clova
Glen Clova is acclaimed as the finest of the Angus glens, famed for its flora and fauna. It combines the austerity of its higher tops with a tranquillity in its lower reaches which could easily be mistaken for an English dale. Glen Clova is Ogilvie country and just up the glen from the village of Clova are the ruins of Clova Castle, an Ogilvie stronghold destroyed by Cromwellian troops in 1650.

If you continue up the glen to Braedownie, the point where Walks 71 and 72 have ended, you will find just to the north-east, the Lair of Aldararie (2728ft/832m). On a flat grassy expanse close to the summit the folk of Glen

Looking past the ruin of Bachnagairn Lodge towards Glen Clova. ▶

The Burn of Gowall from the footbridge above Bachnagairn.   ▶ ▶

Muick, Glen Esk and Glen Clova used to meet to hold their annual Highland Games right up until the end of the last century. Trials of sporting skill of a different kind take place today on Red Craig which dominates Braedownie to the east. For this is a rock-climbing area, especially popular with Dundee climbers. Red Craig also boasts a Pictish dwelling, the Cave of Weems, which is interesting in its unusual use of the natural rock crevices in its construction.

The corries at this end of Glen Clova are very fine. Beyond the Shank of Drumfollow is the much acclaimed Coire Fee, a veritable fairyland of meadows and falls, with Craig Rennet (2443ft/745m) to the north-east. It is well worth hiking up to the Winter Corrie on the west of the Clova. Follow the Gourock Burn which takes you up into a profusion of screes and rugged rocks.

Above the Winter Corrie is Driesh (3106ft/947m). The easiest approach is to cross the bridge over the South Esk just a short way south-south-east of Braedownie and ascend Corrie Farchal, the corrie to the south-east of the Winter Corrie, between Bassies and Driesh. From the Sneck of Farchal at the lip of the corrie, go west to Driesh by following the fence.

Walk 73   Glen Clova to Glen Esk by Ben Tirran
OS 44: 326631 to 445805
15 miles (24km) with 911ft (278m) of ascent

From the village of Clova go steeply up the hill to the north-east, bypassing Loch Brandy (non-alcoholic) to the south. A witch has put a curse on this loch and one day the cliffs above it are going to fall and the ensuing tidal wave will destroy all life in the glen. But it hasn't happened yet, so take a chance.

After some effort you should arrive at the summit of Green Hill (2853ft/870m). From here you can make a

◀ *The old mill at Milton of Clova.*

▲ *A view across the west end of Loch Lee to the start of the hill path to Glen Clova and Inchgrundle.*

▲ *Glenlee, at the west end of Loch Lee. Further up Glen Lee are the Falls of Unich and above that the Falls of Damff, linked by a footpath.*

detour to Ben Tirran (2938ft/896m) by going across the plateau first to the east, then south-east, passing en route the Craigs of Loch Wharral. The plateau is high and somewhat desolate and can present navigational problems in mist.

Continuing towards Glen Esk, proceed by White Hill and the ridge of Muckle Cairn and the steep descent to Inchgrundle. Then follow the track round the north side of Loch Lee. Just before you reach Invermark you pass the graveyard of the pre-Reformation chapel of St Drostan. The church is now a ruin, but was formerly thatched and despoiled by Montrose's soldiers.

Walk 74 Glen Esk and the Lowps o' the Burn
OS 44: 600710 to 593726
1.5 miles (2km)

Glen Esk is a wonderful Angus glen and the Lowps o' the Burn are well worth a visit. The path along the Lowps exits onto the Glen Esk road a short way up from its junction with the B966 at Edzell. It is perhaps easier to find the start of this short scenic walk from the west side of Gannochy Bridge. This bridge over the North Esk dates from 1732 and utilises two great rocks to span the chasm. The private footpath, which is open to the public at their own risk, takes you alongside the magnificent chasm of the Esk. After about a mile the path emerges onto the Glen Esk road just south of the main powerline.

◀ *St Drostan's graveyard, Loch Lee. A gravestone of 1732 for one Al Brown depicts a mask, wheel-cross and crossed spades. Perhaps he was a grave-digger by occupation. At the other end of the loch the path goes uphill to cross to Glen Clova via the south side of Loch Brandy.*

The Lowps o' the Burn and the Rocks of Solitude are part of the magnificent gorge of the North Esk just above Gannochy Bridge near Edzell. The Rocks are upstream, but can be viewed by taking a footpath from the road. ▶

246

Gaelic and Norse Glossary

A	river, stream (Norse).
Aber, Abar	also as: Obar, mouth or confluence of a river.
Abhainn,	also as: Amhainn, river.
Allt	also as: Ald, Alt, Auld, Ault, burn, brook, stream.
Aoineadh	a steep promontory or brae.
Aonach	a height, a ridge.
Ard, Aird	a high point, promontory.
Ath	a ford, also a kiln.
Ay, Ey, I	island (Norse).
Baile	usually Bal, Bali, town, homestead.
Bàn	white, fair.
Bàrr	a point, extremity.
Beag	also as: Beg, little, small.
Bealach	breach, pass, gap, col.
Beinn	also as: Ben, a mountain.
Bidean	summit.
Binnean	also as: Binnein, a pinnacle or little mountain.
Bò (pl. Bà)	cow, cows.
Bruaich	a bank, brae, brim, steep place.
Buidhe	yellow, golden coloured.
Cadh	a pass, steep path.
Cailleach	a nun, old woman, a witch.
Caisteal	castle.
Cam	crooked, bent, one-eyed.
Caol	also as: Caolas, Kyle, strait, firth, narrow.
Càrn	a heap of stones, cairn.
Carr	broken ground.
Ceann	also as: Ken, Kin, head, headland.
Cill, Kil	a cell, church.
Clach	a stone.
Clachan	stones, hamlet.
Cladh	a churchyard, a burying place.
Cnap	a knob, hillock.
Cnoc, Knock	a knoll.
Coill, Coille	a wood, forest.
Coire	Anglicised form: Corrie, a cauldron, kettle, circular hollow.
Corran	a sickle; semi-circular bay.
Creag	also as: Craig, a rock, cliff.
Crioch	boundary, frontier, landmark.
Crò	a sheepfold, pen.
Crom	bent, sloping, crooked.
Cruach	stack, heap, haunch.
Cùl	the back.
Dail	a field.
Dearg	red.
Doire	grove, hollow.
Druim	also as: Drem, Drom, Drum, the back, ridge.
Dobhar	water, a stream.

Dorus	door. Deoch an doruis, a stirrup-cup.
Dubh, Dhubh	black, dark.
Dùn	a fort, castle, heap.
Eagach	notched.
Ear	east.
Eas	a waterfall.
Easach	a cascade.
Eilean	an island.
Fada	long.
Fearn	an alder tree.
Féith	bog, sinewy stream, a vein.
Fiadh	a deer.
Fionn	fair, white.
Gabhar	a goat.
Garbh,	also as: Garve, rough.
Geal	white, clear, bright.
Geodha	a narrow creek, chasm, rift, cove.
Gearanach	a wall-like ridge.
Geàrr	short.
Glais	a stream, burn.
Glas	grey, pale, wan, green.
Gleann	usually Glen, narrow valley, dale, dell.
Gob	point, beak.
Gorm	blue, azure, green.
Gualann	shoulder of mountain or hill.
Lag	usually Lagan, Logie, a hollow in a hill.
Lair	an axe.
Lairig	the sloping face of a hill, a pass.
Leac	a ledge.
Leathad	a slope, declivity.
Leathan	broad.
Leitir	a slope.
Liath	grey.
Linne	pool, sound, channel.
Lòn	a marsh, morass.
Màm	a round or gently rising hill.
Maol	headland, bald top, cape.
Meall	knob, lump, rounded hill.
Monadh, Mounth	moor, heath, hill, mountain.
Mòine	also as: Mointeach, peat-mossland, mossy.
Mór	great, large, tall. Anglicised form: More.
Muileann	mill.
Muir	the sea.
Mullach	a rounded hill.
Rathad	a road, way.
Réidh	plain, level, smooth.

Riabhach	also as: Riach, drab, greyish, brindled, grizzled.
Righ	king.
Ruadh	red, reddish.
Rudha	usually Ru, Rhu, Row, promontory.

Sean	old, aged, ancient.
Sgorr	also as: Sgurr, Scaur, a peak, conical sharp rock.
Sgreamach	rocky.
Sith	a fairy. Sithean, a fairy hillock or knoll.
Sneachd	snow.
Srath, Strath	a wide valley, plain beside a river.
Sròn, Strone	nose, peak, promontory.
Sruth, Struan	a stream, current.
Stac	a steep rock, conical hill (Norse).
Stob	a point.
Stùc	a pinnacle, peak, conical steep rock.
Suidhe	sitting, resting place.

Taigh, Tigh	usually Tay, Ty, a house.
Teallach	a forge.
Tir, Tyr	country, region, land.
Tobar	a well, spring, fountain.
Toll	a hole.
Tom	a hilloch, mound.
Tòrr	a mound, heap, hill.
Tulach	knoll, hillock, eminence. Anglicised forms: Tilly, Tully, Tulloch.

Uachdar	usually Auchter, Ochter, upper land.
Uaine	green.
Uamh	a cave, grave.
Uig	a nook, bay.
Uisge	water, rain.

Index

Walk starting points are in bold type; photographs are indicated by italic numerals.
Allt, Ben, Beinn, Carn, Coire, Creag, Gleann, Loch, River are indexed under the following name.